Full Spectrum Freedom

REWEAVING THE CONTEXT OF FREEDOM

CHARLOTTE OSTERMANN

MotherheartPress

ISBN: 9781732103719

FOREWORD

Full Spectrum Freedom is part two of a series written in FoAm — the elegant combination of words and symbols that helps give both distance from and access to deep, complex and difficult personal experience. In *You, Free* (part one) you were introduced to the fully integrated, free human being

Here, we take a step back from You, Free to consider the dynamics of his becoming. *Full Spectrum Freedom* addresses, in FoAm, the second dimension of freedom: the way.

Table of Contents

"...BY THE AID OF SYMBOLISM, WE CAN
MAKE TRANSITIONS IN REASONING ALMOST
MECHANICALLY BY THE EYE, WHICH
OTHERWISE WOULD CALL INTO PLAY THE
HIGHER FACULTIES OF THE BRAIN . . ."

ALFRED NORTH WHITEHEAD
AN INTRODUCTION TO MATHEMATICS

Introduction

Over and over while learning to speak FoAm (See Appendix I, About FoAm), I made, talking with my hands, the back–and–forth, figure–eight movement that indicates a developing center. That center is the free, integrated human person known as in FoAm.

I saw that not only is the individual having trouble learning to be free, but he then makes a world that is, likewise, compromised in its integrity. Bent and sinful Man generates bent and sin–disposing form, systems, culture—no surprise there. The surprise came later.

I encountered the first person who had trouble understanding FoAm. To make that long story short, I prayed for help communicating it all in some even simpler way. Someone accustomed to moving toward the integration of Self has an experiential database to draw on when offered circles and triangles as symbols for experience. Someone who has not yet begun to perceive that oh, so necessary movement does not.

In calculus we simplify one variable to near–zero to give easier access to the mathematics of a complex dynamic. Christ seemed to have become that 'infinitessimal' element for us—becoming 'as nothing' to save us. I saw that I needed to drop away the

to focus on the movement itself. I didn't immediately comprehend what that even meant visually, verbally, experientially, but just pondered it all prayerfully. I had to find a way to describe the invisible, to help a person without as much sense of the Self understand and trust the process of his own becoming.

The 'Full Spectrum' is a 'step–down transformation' or 'derivative' of the work in *You,Free*. It has yielded surprising new insights about the dynamics by which community, social capital, culture, communication, hierarchies of value, physical health, gift economies, excellent readers and the metaphoric dimension of human being operate. Your self–cultivation draws upon these contexts and then bears fruit *in* these contexts of being

Each chapter, taken in any order, offers an exercise in 'spectrum weaving' for your response. You'll recall the often–repeated message of *You, Free*: your response is the key to growing in freedom. I suggest you do a bit of journaling about the images, thoughts, and associations you have as you read. Then, do the exercise I've offered– often questions to help start the flow of ideas and provoke response.

"ONE WHO HAS HOPE LIVES DIFFERENTLY."

POPE BENEDICT XVI

1. Invisible Territory

I see the goal. It's way over there:

But I'm stuck, here:

There doesn't seem to be a way to move from here to there. I have a great idea. It looks like this:

I'm stuck in reality I can't change. It looks like this:

Between the dense thicket of now, reality, concrete barriers, and stuck–ness, and the attractive, future, idea and lightness, there seems to be an enormous gap. Possibility attracts me, but I perceive no path to it. Realization appeals to me, but, again, there is no way 'there' from 'here'.

That empty territory is like outer space – I can't breathe in it, can't go into it. I can't stay stuck, and I can't move. I need some certainty to take a step, some confidence to go forward. I need hope.

Hope is an atmosphere of assurance filled with paths I can see.

An atmosphere requires a limit or boundary. A visible path requires substance. Certainty requires proof. Confidence requires trustworthiness.

Faith is the substance that builds this path, the evidence that grounds my certainty, the correspondence to the reality of a trustworthy God who holds me in his own boundary while I grow. Faith is not an idea I must reach, across an impossible chasm, but a tiny and growing, actual, emerging way forward.

The substance of Faith grows in and around you to become a context for being: hope. As you move toward the Love who calls you, the path comes into focus just ahead. The territory of your becoming may be invisible but it's not empty! It is filled with supportive structures, pathways, and sign posts. The truth at the origin of all reality is the Word, Christ. Have faith!

EXERCISE

Where are you stuck? What ideals and dreams are you having trouble realizing? What relationships are disconnected, or strained? What paths are you walking right now? Chart it:

STUCK   **MOVING**   **IF ONLY**

Or draw a continuum arrow and map them all:

"THE WORLD IS INDEED FULL OF PERIL,

AND IN IT THERE ARE MANY DARK PLACES;

BUT STILL THERE IS MUCH THAT IS FAIR,

AND THOUGH IN ALL LANDS LOVE IS NOW

MINGLED WITH GRIEF, IT GROWS PERHAPS

THE GREATER."

J. R. R. TOLKIEN
THE FELLOWSHIP OF THE RING

2. Fear of the Dark

There's darkness that, like a black hole, or Shelob's lair, repudiates and destroys light. Then there's darkness that is mystery, unknowing, subconsciousness, and history.

Scripture tells us that, in God there is no darkness at all (1 John 1:5), but also that even in darkness there is light (Psalm 139:12, Psalm 112:4, John 1:5). If you grow afraid of the dark, you'll miss some of God's richest blessings.

Here's a way to imagine the difference:

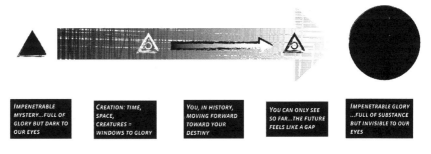

| IMPENETRABLE MYSTERY...FULL OF GLORY BUT DARK TO OUR EYES | CREATION: TIME, SPACE, CREATURES = WINDOWS TO GLORY | YOU, IN HISTORY, MOVING FORWARD TOWARD YOUR DESTINY | YOU CAN ONLY SEE SO FAR...THE FUTURE FEELS LIKE A GAP | IMPENETRABLE GLORY ...FULL OF SUBSTANCE BUT INVISIBLE TO OUR EYES |

Somewhere, long before your history, was a moment when time began. It's completely obscured, or dark, but leads right out to the ever–shining glory of God.

Your destiny—Heaven, eternity, your own purity and divinization—is not an abstract idea, or empty concept, but an attractive and substantial being. The light ahead is substantial, weighty with glory you can't even bear yet. You can't draw that substance, but you've got to learn to see it. Your 'darkness'—the concrete realities of your temporal life, your past, your old scars and brokenness, your deep subconscious needs and yearnings, your lack of awareness or ability — is not darkness–without–light. In fact, it is light cloaked in form, in actuality, in words and things and fact and sometimes–distressing disguises.

Look closely see the light shining through?

Darkness without light looks more like this:

It's dense with lies, knots, black holes and refusal.

If the fabric of your own being becomes knotted like this it can twist your whole being gradually and bend you away from the light.

THINK OF A TWISTING TOWEL . . .
IT REVERSES ON ITSELF

The realities you encounter cast a shadow, and obscure the road ahead.

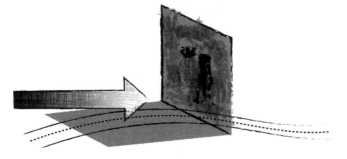

Your emotions cloud and distort your perception.

Failure is confusing, but it teaches you not to demand success. A free act makes no demands.

Avoid sin, evil, error and the confusion they cause. But don't be afraid of the dark.

EXERCISE

Take a look at your past. What are some of the life materials laying around back there? Pivotal memories? Influential people? Big mistakes? "Aha!" moments? Wounds and trauma? Key decisions? Conversions? Reversals? New starts? Failures? Memories of transition, grief, elation, fear? Unrequited love? Healing?

This doesn't have to be a full biography, just take notes of what comes to mind and leave space for more to percolate into your consciousness. For some of the later exercises, this list of practice material may come in handy.

"QUALITY IS NEVER AN ACCIDENT; IT IS
ALWAYS THE RESULT OF INTELLIGENT
EFFORT."

JOHN RUSKIN

3. Learning to See

In a class called *Learning to See by Drawing*, we followed John Ruskin's method. Many little squares were filled with tiny ink cross hatching as we learned the difference between the ideal of "perfect" and the reality of our own work.

FIRST PASS   SECOND PASS   THIRD PASS   FOURTH PASS

'Perfect' is a woven, silk–like texture, of light, even ink marks made in successive, increasingly tedious passes over each square surface. Reality was more of a burlap, knotted with ink blobs and woven of ink strands that varied in texture between 'invisible scratch' to 'double wide swath' (these were usually ugly smudges before the square was done).

PERFECT   ME

'Good Enough' was never good enough. Perfect was the only worthy goal. In fact it was the only reasonable goal—even though it seemed ever farther away.

Good enough did at least give us access to further lessons in representing contour and form with a better-trained eye, hand and pen. The process was deeply centering and seemed to point the soul 'deep' and 'down' into contemplation as the eye and hand attended to pen, paper and ink.

Advanced students graduated to filling long rectangles with ink, seeking a seamless gradation from deep black to ink-free paper-white.

As a not-advanced student, my mind shifted over into verbal at this point. Yes, the work was enjoyable even if impossible, but the idea of the full spectrum was born and made his own demands.

The light I could see in my blocks of 'darkness' reminded me to look not only up and forward, but also down and back for glimpses of God's glory. I could see that the disconnect I had experienced (in myself, in others, in the church) between 'real life' and 'spiritual life', between faith and practice, between truth and form, is the 'positive absence' of a work that needed doing. I need, we need to perfect that whole spectrum, or at least try.

THERE SHOULDN'T
BE A DISCONNECT

'REAL LIFE'   'SPIRITUAL
                      LIFE'

How hard are you willing to work to weave your life as beautifully as possible? Will you strive for perfect, and keep practicing to get the knots, blobs, and smudges out?

Just for fun: draw a few 1" squares on your paper and try filling them, one pass at a time, with perfect penmanship. Try a full spectrum rectangle if you're ambitious. This is a genuinely meditative exercise!

"…WHAT WE HAVE AROUND US IS THE MERE METHOD AND PREPARATION FOR SOMETHING THAT WE HAVE TO CREATE. THIS IS NOT A WORLD, BUT RATHER THE MATERIAL FOR A WORLD. GOD HAS GIVEN US NOT SO MUCH THE COLOURS OF A PICTURE AS THE COLOURS OF A PALETTE. BUT HE HAS ALSO GIVEN US A SUBJECT, A MODEL, A FIXED VISION. WE MUST BE CLEAR ABOUT WHAT WE WANT TO PAINT.…WE MUST BE FOND OF THIS WORLD, EVEN IN ORDER TO CHANGE IT. …WE MUST BE FOND OF ANOTHER WORLD (REAL OR IMAGINARY) IN ORDER TO HAVE SOMETHING TO CHANGE IT TO."

G.K. CHESTERTON
ORTHODOXY

4. Chiastic Formation

Scott Hahn introduced me to the concept of the chiasm: some people, the Hebrews among them, wrote their histories with high or focal points at the center of the narrative, rather than at its culmination. Thus, the story of the Crucifixion might be preceded by the stories of creation and the tribe of Abraham and followed by stories of the Apostles and the apocalypse. Readers would note the parallels on each side as pointing to the Cross as the central focus of this collection.

To follow a chiastic path requires you to hold what has been said in expectancy and tension with what follows. You won't know the main event until you've passed it and begin to sense resonance back and forth between the surrounding parts.

We post–moderns expect a good deal more efficiency in our history writing, and so have succumbed to the awful fallacy that forward motion (in this case chronology) equals progress. That arrow of progress, as we will see, has torn the fabric of human being to shreds. In contrast, you are practicing the back–and–forth, lemniscate movement of chiastic formation by which you are woven together in continuity over time.

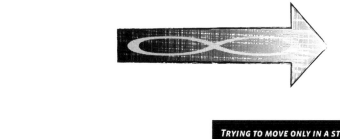

TRYING TO MOVE ONLY IN A STRAIGHT LINE, IF IT DOESN'T DRIVE YOU CRAZY, AT LEAST REDUCES YOUR FREEDOM AND SCOPE OF MOVEMENT.

Though you age only upward, you embrace and integrate all of the temporal dimensions of your becoming. The task is to build up all that actuality into a light–bearing vessel and weave all that light–substance down into actuality. Even your past and your deep subconscious can be mined for gemstones, or used to light new fire within you. You will not become a finished product, but a fully–realized person.

At every point in your journey, you will be a mix of stages—a newcomer to some skills, mature in others; taken seriously as an adult while growing ever more playful and adventurous; floating like a babe in the ocean of divine mercy, and also running like a young Jesse Owens in the path of God's commands. Nothing you ever were, or that you ever experienced is wasted in God's making of You.

Are there any old bits you thought you'd throw out? Offer them to the Artist for use in the beautiful Mosaic that is You.

In what sense, skills, or areas of your life are you a 'child'? A 'youth'? An 'adult'? In what areas do you wish you could be more childlike? More youthful? More mature?

Are there any parts of you that don't seem to have (or to have had) any purpose? This is an important list for later reflection.

"ST. THOMAS CALLED ART 'REASON IN MAKING'. THIS IS A VERY COLD AND VERY BEAUTIFUL DEFINITION, AND IF IT IS UNPOPULAR TODAY, THIS IS BECAUSE REASON HAS LOST GROUND AMONG US. AS GRACE AND NATURE HAVE BEEN SEPARATED, SO IMAGINATION AND REASON HAVE BEEN SEPARATED, AND THIS ALWAYS MEANS AN END TO ART. THE ARTIST USES HIS REASON TO DISCOVER AN ANSWERING REASON IN EVERYTHING HE SEES."

FLANNERY O'CONNOR
MYSTERY AND MANNERS

5. The Arrow of Progress

The arrow of progress is deadly. Aimed at God, it has hit its mark in man, His image. Like all of Satan's tricks, it has a double twist.

First, convince man that God is gone and suck much of the breathable air out of the atmosphere of his becoming. Next, convince him he is or will be God, and he abandons all the structural supports for his own Freedom. More and more impotent to regenerate the context of his being, (religion, family, culture) he is further undermined by the bent and poisoned expressions of his own godhood. Finally, flattened by the burden of slavery to progress, he may succumb to despair.

Consider how different man's destiny looks through the arrow–straight lens:

Of course even those who don't believe it are held in God as they grow. They do cohere over time, in general, and all the elements of their becoming are present, even if not filled with light.

Christianity has contributed mightily to the context they inhabit, even if Christ has been rejected as the interior organizing principle of their lives. His body, the Church, maintains His resounding Presence in the world, so they live in an atmosphere of hope even if they need help taking it in.

The most important difference between these two models is man's place. Either he is the final product, made 'redundant' by tomorrow's new model and technologies he thought were his servants, or he is the radiant, generative center by whose thriving all progress is judged.

Christ is at the origin of his being, whether or not he lives in congruence with that reality.

The arrow, having pierced the atmosphere of hope and left us all gasping, also (and as a result) damaged every sphere of our cultural expression.

Without man–God's–image at its center, education became a factory production line for an ever newer and better human being. If man was now God, education was his savior. That center has, of course, not held. The field is increasingly polarized, with elite educations at one end, and Everyman's at the other. Alas, the ideal of an ennobling education for all was a Christian one with an ideal Man at its origin and a free Man as its goal, or *telos*.

In our care of creation, we're now split between the 'users' and the 'worshippers', waiting for someone to see that man must be the (much more careful and reverent) steward of a creation that serves him — is not his slave or his God. In economics, though we realize our bent institutions are hurting us, we remain at their mercy without the kind of integral human development only free and well integrated human beings can achieve.

Art — last hit, perhaps, by the arrow, has 'progressed' right away from its origin in the Creator and its telos in the heart of man. No longer concerned with its effectiveness as light–bearer, truth–former and way–maker, art often serves men's unmaking.

In every one of these spheres there are also hopeful developments emerging…(drum roll please) from recalibration of 'progress' with greater weight given to its impact on actual, tangible human beings.

Though it may humble us to be slowed somewhat in our individual and collective forward progress, that turning back toward the freedom and well–being of the human person is the key to all truly progressive cultural developments.

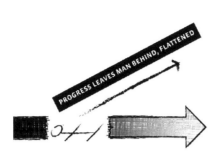

How's the air in your atmosphere? Full of hope, or despair? Ordered or disordered? Calm or clamorous? Opaque or translucent?

Are you at the center of your becoming, or off somewhere making progress? Are you breathing? Moving? Growing? What would it mean for you to return to your own personhood?

"AND HE SHALL BE LIKE A TREE PLANTED BY
THE RIVERS OF WATER, THAT BRINGS FORTH
HIS FRUIT IN HIS SEASON; HIS LEAF ALSO
SHALL NOT WITHER; AND WHATEVER HE
DOES SHALL PROSPER."

PSALM 1:3

6. About Growth

You begin *being* when two cells unite into one, and God greets you deep in the womb. This encounter is like a kiss — your first encounter with reality as You. In this moment, God makes place in his heart for the reality of you. In Him you live and move and have being. Already, small as you are, you cannot bear the fullness of your own self, but must be given place in another person.

Now, with this kiss, the hope is planted in you of attaining the fullness of you — of fully realizing yourself within Him. This is not a hope your tiny self can put into words, or your emotions feel, or your will respond to. It is the hope of your *being*, and it motivates you toward God, toward life, toward freedom from this moment on.

After a brief pause in your growth to rest in Him, you reach out to begin to realize that hope. At the implantation of the tiny blastocyst that is You, a bond is forged with Mother. Little by little, as you encounter reality — assimilating it, being affected by it, responding to it — an 'I' grows: a person with being that is huge, compared to the mere fact of your existence.

So, you yearn toward an ultimate destiny, and on the way you encounter reality and make it your own — you feast on reality! It corresponds to the desire God gave you to possess everything and everyone He created for you — even to possess Him.

YOU IN THE WOMB

YOU, IN THE HOME: WHAT YOU'VE BEEN 'EATING' IS NOW INTERNAL STRUCTURE.

YOU HAVE A VORACIOUS APPETITE FOR REALITY, AND IT'S THE MAKING OF YOU!

The tiny 'I' must, right from the start, appropriate the context, the reality in which it finds itself. That encounter with reality — or a breast, a voice, a word, hard or hot surfaces, a frightening fall — actually becomes the stuff of Self. In your taking–in and incorporating of reality, you are rather like a tree. The personal and social structures you form continue to operate as 'reality processing systems'. Just as the tree's roots, tissues and branches expand in capacity to take in sunlight, carbon dioxide, food, and water and to give out shelter, fruit, wood, and oxygen, you expand to your own personal greatness through the upward spiraling of the seasons.

Spiral growth feels like 'going around in circles,' but is more accurately a 'weaving up in circles.' As the back–and–forth movement adds to You, you rise up to inhabit a much larger space. Sometimes you will be lush with new life – self–expression, culture–building, activity, hospitality, and fruitfulness. At other times, you'll slow in forward, expansive movement to consolidate, build strength, evaluate and re–organize.

You'll out–fill into the world – taking and holding more and more of the territory of Self. Your Self will in–fill with structure that holds and takes in more of the raw material that becomes you.

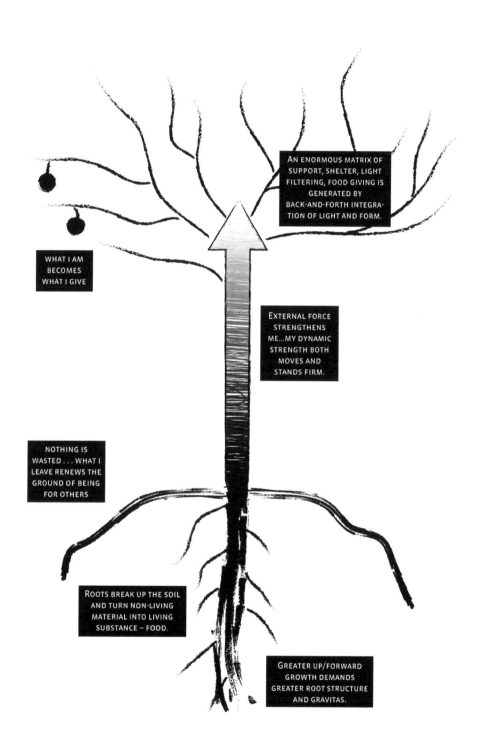

AN ENORMOUS MATRIX OF SUPPORT, SHELTER, LIGHT FILTERING, FOOD GIVING IS GENERATED BY BACK-AND-FORTH INTEGRATION OF LIGHT AND FORM.

WHAT I AM BECOMES WHAT I GIVE

EXTERNAL FORCE STRENGTHENS ME...MY DYNAMIC STRENGTH BOTH MOVES AND STANDS FIRM.

NOTHING IS WASTED . . . WHAT I LEAVE RENEWS THE GROUND OF BEING FOR OTHERS

ROOTS BREAK UP THE SOIL AND TURN NON-LIVING MATERIAL INTO LIVING SUBSTANCE – FOOD.

GREATER UP/FORWARD GROWTH DEMANDS GREATER ROOT STRUCTURE AND GRAVITAS.

Draw some concentric circles and label them in correspondence with the context of your being. For example:

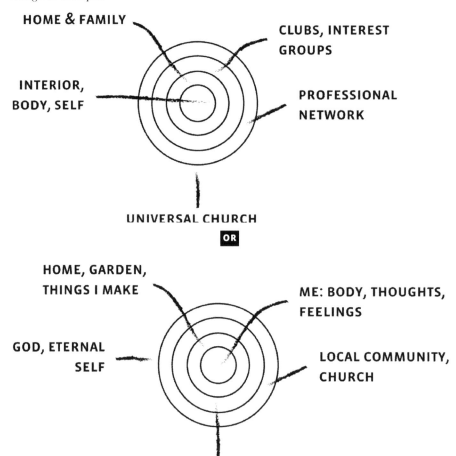

HOME & FAMILY

CLUBS, INTEREST GROUPS

INTERIOR, BODY, SELF

PROFESSIONAL NETWORK

UNIVERSAL CHURCH

OR

HOME, GARDEN, THINGS I MAKE

ME: BODY, THOUGHTS, FEELINGS

GOD, ETERNAL SELF

LOCAL COMMUNITY, CHURCH

FAMILY AND FRIENDS

For fun practice those pen skills, shading this from dark to light. Keep these contexts in mind as you go forward.

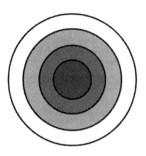

"I THOUGHT,' SHE SAID, 'THAT I WAS CARRIED IN THE WILL OF HIM I LOVE, BUT NOW I SEE THAT I WALK WITH IT. I THOUGHT THAT THE GOOD THINGS HE SENT ME DREW ME INTO THEM AS THE WAVES LIFT THE ISLANDS; BUT NOW I SEE THAT IT IS I WHO PLUNGE INTO THEM WITH MY OWN LEGS AND ARMS, AS WHEN WE GO SWIMMING....IT IS A DELIGHT WITH TERROR IN IT!"

C. S. LEWIS
PERELANDRA

7. Tense and Tension

If your path through time (chronos) looks like this:

Kairos (God's time outside time) looks like this:

It should be much bigger, of course, as it's infinite. It dwarfs the finite time–path you are on. The entire space–time continuum would be just a drop in the bucket of kairos, and you are just one tiny thread in its weave!

This movement, in you,

is participation in the movement of the Holy Spirit.

Your imagination can time travel to some extent, but you should realize that, as a conceptual exercise, it threatens to disintegrate you from the realities you actually face. If you had no imaginative capacity, you might find yourself stuck in and overwhelmed by the present. Especially in youth, the present seems to insist on being taken as the whole of reality — unshackled to the past and unrelieved by a hopeful future. Youth can be a very myopic phase. The work of growing up and growing better integrated includes the development of awareness that you exist in three tenses at once, and of acceptance of the present moment as the only tense in which you can act.

Past and future form the 'context' of the present, where the 'content' that is You coheres over time. Your past, with all its incorporation into your brain, your body, your story, continues as you move toward your eternal destiny. Christ has set you free, so you are free indeed. Christ is realized in your fully–realized, free personhood and in His body, the Church. You participate in the process of his realization by your own becoming.

In the movement between Christ–in–you and Christ–in–His–Church, between act and being acted upon, between Self and others, you are acquiring, practicing, appropriating freedom. One day, you will have become perfectly and eternally free.

The invitation to freedom is for now. Since grace can only be present to you now, You, Free must be present now to whatever reality you face. To try to project yourself into the future is futile. To hold on to the past is futile. But God holds them for you. Trusting Him to do so, to hold You in coherence over time, is the opposite of futility: faith.

How well–connected are you with your past? How hard was it to mine your past for life materials in Chapter 2? Is there anything back there that you feel must stay put and not trouble your 'now'?

Look forward in time as far as you can. How far did you go?

What's the longest promise you've ever made and kept? For what span of time have you been you–as–you–are–now? Do you have any sense of your ancestry, heritage, place in history, or ethnic background?

For fun: draw a timeline of your life.

"CONVERSATION IS THE CONTEXT OF TRUTH."

JOSEF PIEPER
IN TUNE WITH THE WORLD

FULL SPECTRUM FREEDOM | 40

8. Your Standing Wave

In *You, Free* I introduced you to your vagus nerve. There we saw the possibility of getting stuck in one of two opposite self–protective reactions (fight–or–flight, or collapse). The opposite of this frozen–in–un–freedom is the fluidity of full spectrum freedom.

If you have good vagal tone, you have access to the full spectrum of responses to reality. If you don't, you have an increasingly limited repertoire of responses. The more loss of full spectrum, the harder it is to hold on to what's left, or to recover equilibrium.

**DECREASE IN CONTINUITY = GREATER POLARIZATION;
TENDENCY TO DISINTEGRATION = LESS RESPONSE-ABILITY.**

Instead of a string tuned to its one perfect note, the vagus nerve is like a standing wave within you that resonates with subtle cues about whether you are safe, loved, in danger of physical or emotional harm, trusting reasonably, or being fully seen and heard. The more you experience 'danger,' (and remember, it is your body registering the sense of danger, not your mind, and not your emotions) the less able you may be to open yourself to encounter with reality.

Your boundary closes in self–defense, or you relinquish Self to survive. You begin to anticipate what you've experienced before, bracing against its compressive force without noticing the impact of that constriction upon your interior dimension.

Full spectrum freedom is about reweaving the full physical, emotional, intellectual, spiritual, and social context of your being, where neglect or trauma or misinformation or sin or self–defense have left gaps. Rebuilding your full range of vagal tone is a support for your overall well–being and a great metaphor for your freedom.

Let's consider five possible vagal states:

1. SYMPATHETIC ACTIVATION

Something has triggered the adrenaline surge and muscle tension of your fight–or–flight response (sympathetic nervous system activation by a fear trigger). If this state persists after actual danger has passed, you find yourself hyper–aware, narrowly focused on some one goal, or element of reality, or on your mental rehearsal of the narrative of this experience. You need help to take in more of reality, to diffuse your focus, to relax. The resilient, 'well–woven' vagus acts as a brake on sympathetic action, by activating the parasympathetic relaxation response.

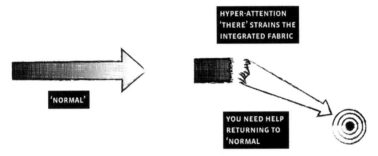

To help yourself out of this state when you don't need it to save a life, try this:

PRAYER (OF COURSE): "Perfect Love, cast out fear!"

DEEP SLOW BREATHING: Imagine it filling your whole torso; Inhale through your nose; Release your diaphragm; Hold for a moment before exhaling; Hold for a moment before inhaling.

SENSORY ENGAGEMENT: Fill your senses with aroma, music, taste, texture, temperature change, visual beauty.

SOCIAL ENGAGEMENT: Enter the presence of someone who makes eye contact, nods sympathetically, and has a voice with warmth and feeling in it. Ask for help, hugs, a listening ear, a word of encouragement, a cup of tea.

SLOW TO A STOP: Change your reactive race to a reflective pace.

2. DORSAL VAGAL COLLAPSE

Something has overwhelmed your safety circuit and you've gone limp in its jaws. This is the parasympathetic system's emergency response. If this state occurs with no actual present danger, it may be a residue of past trauma, a habitually slack and impotent response, a ducking of responsibility, an untenable situation (literally a tension you cannot bear), or fatigue from too much time spent fighting and fleeing reality in a habitually hyper–mobilized self–protection.

Do you feel confused? Are your facial muscles, neck, or shoulders tight? Are you holding your breath? You become less able to think in words and to process the human voice just when you need them most. You need help to re–discover your own freedom, to articulate the details, to recover a 'forward and upward' orientation.

To help yourself out of this state when you perceive it does not correspond to the current reality, try this:

PRAYER: always the first thing — is even more important when you are in this essentially powerless state. You may actually have no resources available with which to help yourself.

SOCIAL ENGAGEMENT: Human interaction is tonic — helping you back from either extreme reaction to anxiety to the center where you find peace, equilibrium and freedom. We really do need each other. Without help, we tend to resort to self–regulation by stuff– and–substances.

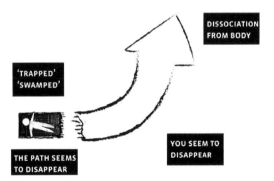

GET WORDS: Start with God's. Also helpful is formal prayer, journaling about the situation, the sound of your own voice can help you recover vagal equilibrium.

LIGHT–VOLUME NASAL BREATHING: It is possible to 'over–breathe' yourself into a too–down–regulated state. Try taking in less air, through your nose (to send nitric oxide through your vascular system), down into your relaxed abdomen without effort or chest/shoulder engagement, and waiting a bit longer after exhalation. See how long you can feather out air when you exhale (it helps to imagine a feather floating gently downward).

ACT, MOVE, DANCE, WALK, JUMP: Get your heart beating a bit faster to upregulate vagal tone.

BITTERS: A quick spray of herbal bitters has a tonic effect on vagal tone. See if it helps you.

3. INTIMACY AND SOLITUDE

The down–regulation of vagal tone enables you to be immobilized, but without the fear that triggers collapse and dissociation. This is part of the 'sweet spot' of freedom. The well–woven vagal 'fabric' allows for this sharing of the boundary of self. Intimacy involves some interior tension, so it both challenges and rewards your freedom.

To be truly at leisure is to be free just to be yourself, alone or with a loved one. Notice how you feel when in intimate human contact. Do you begin to breathe faster or experience abdominal tension, as though you're frightened? Do you feel somewhat pinned or trapped? Do you feel the rising tension of conflicting hopes, demands, needs, moods, values, or thoughts? Is stillness hard for you to bear? Silence?

Pray for God's help to up– or down–regulate your vagal responses as you sense these flutters in your equilibrium. They are natural, but can interfere with intimacy. Supernatural power is available to help you grow in your capacity to remain present without fear. Full spectrum freedom does not pretend there never is danger, but is ready to respond appropriately to whatever reality is actually encountered — to correspond to rather than react to reality is freedom.

4. WORK AND PLAY

To be able to mobilize yourself without the stimulus of fear, or from an internal locus of control, is freedom. The up–regulation of vagal tone enables the conscious, free exercise of will by which both effective work and enjoyable play are both characterized. Teamwork, or play, is an extension of the social engagement that is tonic to good vagal function. The full spectrum of that functionality is woven of the actualities of your life. The strands of experience act as vessels for intention, value, meaning, or light. The strands of words act as scaffolding for the lived encounter with reality, becoming poetry, wisdom, narrative.

Through the imaginative faculty, verbal structures help lay straight paths for your feet as you move forward and up toward your eternal destiny. Experience enters the actual fibers of your being as scar tissue, fascial knots, tender spots and habits both physical and emotional.

Your work and play may accomplish near goals and far, products and pleasure, sweat and satisfaction. They also accomplish You. There is a natural oscillation even in a free, well–balanced, integrated human being between 'up' and 'down,' 'activation' and 'rest'. Your body (and your Sabbath!) is designed with your wholeness in mind.

5. THE SWEET SPOT

If there was a perfect mix of intimacy and activity, it might be conversation. The experience of a great conversation is a picture of well integrated, full spectrum freedom. In it, free individuals relinquish their separate boundaries for the greater good of this union. In it we play with words and ideas for pure pleasure, even if it takes a lot of work to orchestrate and prepare for the fun. There, truth finds its context as words are woven into vessels for light. There, light finds its form as we struggle to share our thoughts and experience in words.

Good vagal tone is actually vital to a good conversation. We must feel safe to entrust ourselves fully to this group, and to bear the tension of the oscillation between intimate vulnerability and sharing that builds community, and playful sparring and challenging by which 'iron sharpens iron'. A conversation, very like the fabric of being involves contextual trust and richness, worthy and well–articulated content, and back–and–forth movement to become fully woven. Such a conversation is at once the great reward and the great promoter of full spectrum vagal tone.

Do you tend to be 'too slack,' 'too taut,' or 'just right'? Have you ever experienced collapse, depression, shut down, or dissociation? Have you ever experienced hostile speed, unexplained panic, sheer terror, or fantasies of beating someone up? Have you ever had a sense of danger, without knowing what triggered it? Have you ever felt you were not safe to be, or to be the 'real you' in someone's presence?

What's the most satisfying hard–work, or hard–play experience you've ever had? What's the most enjoyable social experience you've ever had?

If you could pull together a great conversation for a few people, who would you pick to join you?

"JESUS TOOK PETER, JAMES AND JOHN WITH HIM AND LED THEM UP A HIGH MOUNTAIN TO PRAY. AS HE WAS PRAYING, HE WAS TRANSFIGURED BEFORE THEM. HIS FACE SHONE LIKE THE SUN, AND HIS CLOTHES BECAME DAZZLING WHITE, AS WHITE AS THE LIGHT, AS BRIGHT AS A FLASH OF LIGHTNING."

MATTHEW 17:1–8, MARK 9:2–8, LUKE 9:28–36

9. Step–Down Transformation

We need full spectrum electricity that ranges from 345,000 Volts at the electric power plant to 120 Volts at our toaster plug–in. One way to look at full spectrum freedom is through this lens.

In a full spectrum freedom, there is an unbroken continuum between end and means, origin and telos, vessel and value, form and meaning, temporal experience and eternal destiny. The natural stuff of the weave is the actuality of experience, act, form, and word. The supernatural stuff is the meaning, value, revelation and illumination carried into form. All that could look like this:

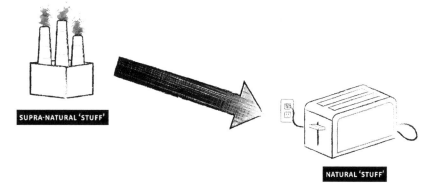

SUPRA-NATURAL 'STUFF'

NATURAL 'STUFF'

From encounter with reality we accumulate a collection of building blocks. Like kids playing with Legos, we configure and reconfigure them to build out into the world – paths, shelters, beautiful patterns, buildings and bridges. These are the mediating structures by which space is supported, power is delivered, sound is communicated throughout the Self.

A lightning strike could move destructively through the linked structures. If electricity is to be delivered, it must stop here and there to be transformed in potency, lest it be damaging. The story of Moses, peeking from the cleft of a rock as God passed in His glory (See Exodus 33:22) demonstrates that man may not directly perceive the full glory of God without suffering harm. Thus, That glory is mediated to us through creation, through Christ, and through verbal structures (such as Liturgy, doctrine, Scripture, mythology), where it is variously veiled.

Similarly, the immense *Summa Theologica* of St Thomas Aquinas has been step–down transformed in books such as Peter Kreeft's *Summa of the Summa*. Our Lord is transmitted through consecrated Bread and Wine. Light's energy is transformed into edible matter by the mediation of plants. The continuum of the whole fabric of being is woven of mediating structures that collect, transform, then translate its content. The same power that holds all being in coherence then illuminates and resounds through it. Love desires to weave you into integration, to radiate through you the invitation to freedom, and to speak with your voice.

If freedom is power to act, as electricity is power to activate a circuit then freedom implies *means*. Form, word, act: the means, or mediating structures, in which Super–Reality is reduced, stepped down, hidden, veiled, *and* given, distributed, communicated.

You are rising up in virtue, strength, structural capacity, to meet, to receive, to transform and transmit the call of your destiny, the gifts of God. You are rising up to meet, to connect with, to plug into lightning itself! Get ready. Get free!

Sometimes it's hard to see change in yourself unless you look back over a longer period. Set your gaze back far enough to register some difference, and write about some of the ways you've changed in those 5, 10, or 30 years. What do you think about the overall direction of that change? Are there any strands that seem to be pulling the whole fabric 'out of true'?

Now look ahead, but not too far. Where do you want to see change in yourself 3 – 5 years from now? Be specific about what you want, and why. Next, describe the obstacles that stand between you and those hoped–for changes.

"HE IS COMING FOR ME, THE ONE IN WHOM
I WILL BE WHAT I SHOULD BE AND WOULD
LIKE TO BE. ...I SHIFT THE CENTRAL POINT,
THE MAIN EMPHASIS OF MY SELF OUT OF MY
EPHEMERAL, DECAYING PRESENT INTO HIS
PROMISED FUTURE, GUARANTEED AS CERTAIN
THROUGH HIS CROSS AND RESURRECTION.
...A SELF CAN IN THE END BE FOUND AND
SHELTERED ONLY IN A LOVING THOU. ...THE
DEFINITIVE LAW OF BEING..."

HANS URS VON BALTHASAR
CONVERGENCES

10. Hierarchy of Value

'Hierarchy' is a much–maligned term. Though it just means a clear, top–down governance structure, it has come into disfavor in our egalitarian times. Hierarchy, or vertical governance, can operate in good relationship with more 'organic,' or two–way systems and communication. In fact, today's management textbooks are filled with examples of successful organizations transformed by this more integrated approach.

In the post–Enlightenment years when man began pretending God didn't exist and all people could be made equal by education, it began to seem snobbish, aristocratic, and old–fashioned to speak of 'higher things', 'highest qualities', and transcendent values. While 'mass man' was democratized, homogenized and flattened by an education system no longer concerned with setting him free, the highest things also devolved into elitism, popularity, privilege, power and wealth.

We can still speak of the top qualities of the five–star Chef, the $200–per–bottle wine, the million–dollar basketball player, or the contest–winning pianist. We acknowledge and revere great skill or great accomplishment. We don't as often see great moral goodness, or great skill in truth–telling lauded. The 'top' isn't gone. The bar has just been lowered to what man can accomplish on his own, without revelation, or grace. Interestingly, as the bar lowered, the gap widened. The goal became more and more material, and Everyman's access to higher things decreased.

Granted many notable exceptions to the overall pattern (some sense of *noblesse oblige* among the rich still keeps art museums open, for instance) when you see it as a pattern you can also see a way of recovery. We need a higher hierarchy, not a pretense that a compass can choose its own 'true north'. It's not enough to raise the bar. We must also make a way. If the hierarchy of value extends all the way to the heights, those who can attain those heights must intend to turn back and make for others a path of approach. Thus will a richly woven context develop to support each person toward His highest possibilities.

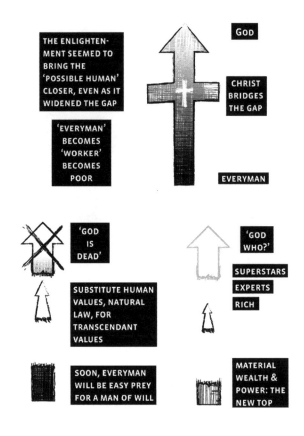

THE ENLIGHTEN-
MENT SEEMED TO
BRING THE
'POSSIBLE HUMAN'
CLOSER, EVEN AS IT
WIDENED THE GAP

'EVERYMAN'
BECOMES
'WORKER'
BECOMES
POOR

GOD

CHRIST
BRIDGES
THE GAP

EVERYMAN

'GOD
IS
DEAD'

SUBSTITUTE HUMAN
VALUES, NATURAL
LAW, FOR
TRANSCENDANT
VALUES

SOON, EVERYMAN
WILL BE EASY PREY
FOR A MAN OF WILL

'GOD
WHO?'

SUPERSTARS
EXPERTS
RICH

MATERIAL
WEALTH &
POWER: THE
NEW TOP

Look back at the lists you made in Chapter 4. For each of those 'adult' or 'mature' areas, or capabilities, consider how you might turn to offer them to a younger or less–skilled person. For example, if you play the piano at an adult level, how could you share that skill with someone who can't play?

Now consider your 'child' list. For each one, think of someone who models the adult version you're aiming for. For example, if you know nothing about car repair, and your dad keeps the whole family fleet running, or you're scared to travel and your kids have toured Europe successfully. Think about how you might ask for help, insight, tips, lessons or a reading plan to get you moved further into that territory of Self on this particular path.

"...WHEN THE SON BECAME MAN, HE DID NOT ABOLISH CREATION'S LAW OF DAY AND NIGHT. INSTEAD, HE SIMPLY LED IT BEYOND ITSELF BY BRINGING THE LIGHT OF GOD, SO THAT, WITH IT, HE COULD FIGHT AGAINST THE DARKNESS OF HELL; HE COULD BREAK THROUGH ITS NIGHT WITH THE RADIANCE OF THIS LIGHT, NOT SIMPLY TO CHASE DARKNESS OUT OF THE WORLD, BUT TO FILL IT WITH A WEALTH OF DIVINE MEANING."

ADRIENNE VON SPEYR
LIGHT AND IMAGES

11. Metaphor is a Way

With metaphors we make a link between two things—a path where there was a gap between them. In its way, a metaphor weaves new meaning into one form by joining it to another. It's a quick way to get from 'here' to 'there.'

To rebuild the way, to refill the context, of becoming, we need to develop a stronger metaphorical sense.* Every verbal structure, every field of study, every avenue of communication needs the 'oxygen' of metaphor to thrive.

The pathways, and man's 'anagogical sense' are missing because of the disintegration of persons. Man is further reduced by life in the vacuum he has created.

How do you work in metaphor to restore the continuous fabric of being?

STEP ONE: **HONOR IT**

Metaphor has been dethroned as the highest and deepest means by people whose one–way arrows point only away from the poetic intelligence and language of 'the old days' toward the scientific, or academic mode. Academic speech is dispassionate, dry, analytical; designed to be received by the intellect; full of proof, logic, definitions, footnotes, and assertions; dependent on a long train of experience with a body of work, or field of study; aims at efficiency, but seems an impenetrable thicket of redundance to outsiders. For many, credentials are the whole aim of word use:

SCHOOL-SPEAK IN THE PERSPECTIVE
OF A RICH SPECTRUM OF WORD WEAVING

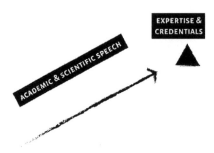

EXPERTISE &
CREDENTIALS

ACADEMIC & SCIENTIFIC SPEECH

Note that the 'school–speak' of academia is a reduction from the lively interplay in words that is characteristic of active intellects. It has been flattened from a much richer spectrum of whole–person communication. In the context of the whole human person, or whole society, if we get stuck in a merely verbal use of words, we lose the whole spectrum of possibility.

So, first, stop thinking of metaphor as childish, as primitive, as old fashioned!

STEP TWO: **INGEST METAPHOR**

You are what you eat! Read poetry (preferably aloud), Scripture (Jesus spoke in parables because metaphor is the most excellent way, not because his listeners were stupid), excellent literature (Tolkien's *Lord of the Rings* is a masterpiece of way–building for human beings in the desert of post Christian modernity).

STEP THREE: **LOOK FOR A GAP, START WITH A WORD**

A gap, a chasm, a void, a vacuum, a disconnect is a something–that–is–not. Like a gaping wound, it is a negative space where a positive closure is needed. Like scar tissue, the words by which you articulate the reality you face begin to lay down a matrix of reweaving, where new living cells may take hold and grow.

My first word, when the gap is between persons, is 'unity'. Without any cooperation from another person, I am free — by the virtue of the Holy Spirit — to establish with him an essential unity. The metaphor that comes to mind is 'lifeline,' and by it I change the void to a participation in the Spirit's work of blessing that person. Once I am tethered to another person, they have a place in my heart and prayer. The 'lifeline' becomes an 'I.V.', an 'oxygen mask', an 'electric cord', or even a 'growing placenta' between us. Whatever the metaphor, the place formed by unity can be filled with love.

When the gap is between my mind and something I don't understand, the metaphor is simply 'path' or 'bridge' I need definitions, a simplified explanation, the grammar of the subject, or a good teacher to lead me through the territory of Not–Knowing.

A gap often shows up between the mind and body, or intellect and emotions, especially when the experience of pain is being avoided. Look for metaphors that help you reconnect verbally to physical and emotional experience. Look at the words and images you are using to describe your experience. What do they tell you?

This pain is …a devouring beast? A dark cave? A boulder? A child making demands?

I'm stuck in… a tiny triangle? My head? A prison? A rut? An endless do–loop?

I am… a dry sponge? A runaway train? A soap opera? An idiot? A pariah? A vending machine?

These images help you to voice what you need next.

I need… a champion to fight for me? A lamp? A pickaxe? An opening principle? A long soak? A break? A new script?

Once you have some verbal connection to what you are experiencing, you can further articulate the path of restoration to full freedom. Remember that it always moves back and forth, weaving back together the self and other, the mind and heart, the past and present, the concrete reality and the conceptual ideal.

If you find yourself moving only one way, you aren't weaving anymore. (You're probably Trying Hard to make progress…ugh!) A little bit of new light should enter your narrative with every pass. A little bit of new verbal structure should rise with every pass. You may find your narrative needs a complete rebuild as further illumination reveals its flaws. If it resists this organic growth, it may have become mere self–defense. Like rigid scar tissue, or proud flesh, your metaphoric scaffolding may get in your way if true freedom is not your goal. Let the next pass of the Holy Spirit untie the knots, loosen the weave, and break off the cast.

God's intention is to set you free, indeed!

Note: These thoughts appear with further development as Education for Freedom, *Newman Society Journal, 12/7/17*

The exercise is in the chapter: how would you finish those sentences?

"My pain is…, I'm stuck in… I am…, I need…"

If you have trouble coming up with metaphors, just give literal answers. Your 'analogical sense' may be a bit rusty.

In Chapter 1, did you think of any relationships with 'gaps'? I encourage you to stop and pray, simply, "Holy Spirit, please establish and strengthen my unity with _____," for each person on that list. Don't try hard to become best friends, just hold your end of the unity string gently and entrust the other end to the Spirit. Release all interior demand about what happens in those relationships. Interior demand is the enemy of You, Free.

"...THERE IS SOMEONE IN WHOM THE ELEMENTS OF OUR EXISTENCE, WHICH ARE CAST FORTH, LOST, WASTED IN THE EMPTINESS OF TIME AND THE IMPERSONAL SPACE, ARE BROUGHT TOGETHER — IN THEIR COMPLETE DEFICIENCY, THEIR POWERLESSNESS AND THEIR FAILURE... WHERE WILL I MEET THIS HEALED, WHOLE SELF THAT I WILL BE? ... IN THE THOU, THE THOU OF GOD THE FATHER, WHO LOVES ME AND HAS THE HEALED, WHOLE IMAGE OF ME FROM ALL ETERNITY. ...THERE, WITH THE GUARANTEE OF PERFECT AUTHENTICITY AND TRUSTWORTHINESS, WE ARE THE PERFECTED WORK FOR GOD THE FATHER, WHICH HE HAD IN HIS MIND FROM THE BEGINNING. IT IS IN THE THOU, THEN, THAT WE FIND OUR I."

HANS URS VON BALTHASAR
CONVERGENCES

12. Figure–Ground Shift

 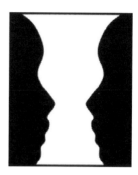

If you see the old lady, you can't see the young one. If you see the faces, you lose the vases. Your eye is seeing both figure and ground, but you're mind locks in on one image at a time. As you journey toward your destiny, or move into the unknowable future, or approach God in prayer, you rise from the ground of being.

When you see the continuum, or don't see the distant future, you feel as though the 'white arrowhead' is empty of content. If we drew it 'full', it would just look like concrete actuality, or impenetrable mystery, but it is full of substantial light. Draw that!

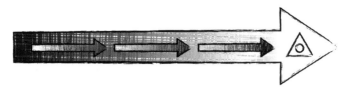

That fullness is, in a sense, emerging through the 'ground' of your 'life materials'. Those materials are your physical substance, your experiences, relationships, thoughts, and the interior infrastructure of the words you're made of. At the same time the light substantial is making itself known, seen, heard, and formed through You, You are raising form, blood and bone, created forms, You, up into the light you are destined to inhabit forever. Notice the shape you take at the end...You, Free: (a spacious, radiant person draped in a complex, beautiful garment)!

The emptiness–that–is–fullness can sometimes cause the equivalent figure–ground shifting of an optical illusion. There's no illusion to it though! You grow more and more able to perceive the super–reality that is permeating your natural actuality. At the same time you grow more aware of the coherent self that is emerging over time, despite detours, organic changes, a swinging pendulum, and the ongoing need for recovery of and growth in freedom. You won't fully see the eternal You until you've cast off the cocoon of time, but you get confusing glimpses.

If you try to walk forward 'by sight,' you'll begin taking steps that are not congruent with the huge swath of Reality you aren't facing. To walk, instead, 'by faith' is to believe that God works in you to will and to do the right things *(Philippians 2:13)*, guides your steps *(Psalm 37:23)*, makes the path straight *(Proverbs 3:6)*, lights your way *(Psalm 119:105)*, gives you reliable teachers *(Ephesians 4:11)*, fights against those who would deter you *(Deuteronomy 20:4)*, accompanies you *(Psalm 23:4)*, died to free you from sin's fabric–twisting effects *(John 8:36)*, feeds you His own perfect Body to sustain you *(Luke 22:19–20)*, protects your Church from error *(Matthew 16:17–19)*, sends angels to serve you *(Hebrews 1:14)*, has plans to prosper you *(Jeremiah 29:11)*, puts words in your mouth *(Isaiah 51:16)*, prays for you when you have no idea what to pray *(Romans 8:26)*, provides loving discipline *(Proverbs 3:12)*, shapes you like a potter molds clay *(Isaiah 64:8)*, and delights in you *(Psalm 18:19)*.

In the moments of confusion between what He's doing and what you're to do, between what you thought the lens was going to be like and what really happens, between good things that can't seem to be reconciled, you are seeing a both–and that you can't resolve. It would be easy to run to one pole or the other, or to plant yourself in one unmoving frame of reference, but this is the adventure of the 'narrow way,' where only God can keep you! (In *3D Freedom*, we'll get into the big reason there is so much turbulence when you are doing the work of becoming free.)

Rather than stare at the Sun, and rather than fixating on the ground at your feet, make it your aim to look toward God for resolution of this paradox. Your own mind can resolve binocular vision into an image but only his tri–nocular vision is adequate to accomplish the amazing both–and that is You, Free. Christ is the metaphor, the Way that brings your figure and ground into perfect focus.

EXERCISE

When have you walked 'by faith'? When have you walked 'by sight'? When have you felt confused about which path to take, which narrative frame to believe in, which competing reality to focus on? What was your heart's desire in each instance? What did you relinquish?

"...WITHOUT SILENCE, WORDS LOSE
THEIR MEANING."

HENRI NOUWEN

13. Full Spectrum Voice

Your voice is a great full–spectrum metaphor. It's designed to make a wide variety of tones, from low to high, loud to soft, fast to slow. In some cultures and some music ensembles men sing soprano and women sing bass. The languages and music of the world reflect the amazing spectrum of vocal possibility.

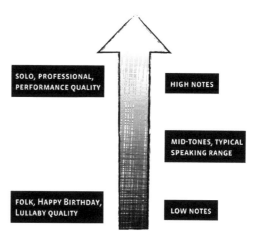

Yet you probably use only a narrow part of that range. You stopped playing with all the sounds you could make when you were a child. You were immersed in only one native language. You sang only with singers in a narrow range, or didn't sing at all. You may even have convinced yourself you were tone deaf (not true for 99% of you).

Your conversational, speaking, reading aloud voice may be the only one you use. If you never allow it to be expressive, passionate, emotional, and animated, your vocal spectrum narrows even more. If your posture is poor, your breathing labored or shallow, your hearing compromised, your vocal usage habits full of tension and interference, the gap widens between actuality and potential.

A flat or deadened vocal pattern is even characteristic of depression and other mental health diagnoses. To be free is to find your voice, to make your full, true sound in this world, to move freely in the whole territory of your being. Your full-spectrum voice provides for others the context of trust, goodwill, safety, and compassion. With your expressive face, voice generates the social engagement by which human beings co-regulate vagal tone in one another.

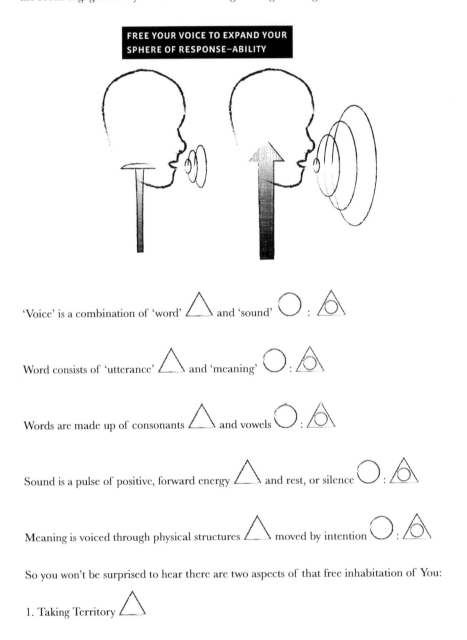

FREE YOUR VOICE TO EXPAND YOUR SPHERE OF RESPONSE–ABILITY

'Voice' is a combination of 'word' △ and 'sound' ◯ : △

Word consists of 'utterance' △ and 'meaning' ◯ : △

Words are made up of consonants △ and vowels ◯ : △

Sound is a pulse of positive, forward energy △ and rest, or silence ◯ : △

Meaning is voiced through physical structures △ moved by intention ◯ : △

So you won't be surprised to hear there are two aspects of that free inhabitation of You:

1. Taking Territory △

Use your life materials to build — upward, forward — vessels that offer openness, receptivity, capacity. Start filling the gap with words and metaphor. Words are your building blocks. The organizing principle is 'Word'.

2. Dwelling Richly

In this case, the opening principle is 'sound'. Open your mouth and make sound. Your voice may also begin to develop in writing, but here we're talking about making actual sound. As you build capability, enjoy your voice more. Consider more and more the meaning of the words being carried on sound. Are you singing along to lyrics that lie? Are your sounds lifting your heart?

Every rip you perceive in the fabric of your being is a missing sound, an unspoken word. What story waits to be told? What pain needs expression? Have you lost your voice?

Draw a large continuum arrow and place each of these elements where you think it belongs. Then, pick a little symbol, or highlight color for Self, and add it to all the places you find yourself along the spectrum you've created. Where are there gaps for you? Which are you interested in closing?

Here are the 'locations' for you to map on your own arrow:

Play with sounds. Study music formally. Folk tunes. Rounds. Silly songs. Child sound. Play with foreign accents. Read aloud. Sing along to CDs. Study vocal technique. Good posture. Breath support. Emotional content. Gregorian chant. High notes. Low notes. Mid–tones. Hum. Sing the Divine Office. Worship music. Classical music. Passion. Music therapy. Popular music. Men's voice. Women's voice. Choral music. Hymns. Liturgical music. Teaching. Counseling. Information exchange. Angelic music. Learn foreign languages. Patriotic music. Whistling. Instrumental music. Acoustic music. Electronic music. Concert. Solo performance. Music theatre. Making animal sounds. Speaking up. Making a speech. Voice–over work. Depressed voice. Happy voice. Angry voice. Sad voice. Business voice. Evangelism. Proclamation. Drill seargent.

Add other vocal possibilities you experience, or notice.

"NOW YOU CAN MAKE REPARATION, "REPAIR"
(THIS IS WHAT THE WORD REPARATION
MEANS). GOD GIVES YOU A MYSTERIOUS
NEEDLE AND THREAD, WITH WHICH YOU
CAN REPAIR THE SEAMLESS GARMENT OF THE
CHURCH TORN BY US SINNERS....WE OFFER
OURSELVES AS THE NEEDLE, THE THREAD,
THE PATCH – FOR OTHERS. WE REALIZE
JUST A LITTLE WHAT IT MEANS TO BE A
MEMBER OF THE MYSTICAL BODY OF CHRIST.
..."THROUGH HIM, WITH HIM, IN HIM," WE
TOO CAN REDEEM THE WORLD."

CATHERINE DOHERTY
THE PEOPLE OF THE TOWEL AND WATER

14. Thick and Thin

If a continuous fabric could be woven that varied from thick–and–coarse opacity to fine–as–silk translucence, it would better illustrate our 'continuum arrow,' and the fabric of being.

The air used to be thick with prayer, church bells, laughter, poetry, stories, conversation, courtesy, children's voices, acoustic music, shared values, the smells of incense, flowers and baking bread. Literature was thick with orality, metaphor, convention, allusion, stock responses, vocabulary, meaning, and invention. Time was thick with history, place, memory, wheels turning within wheels, tradition, story. Eyes beheld and held you, reflected you back to yourself with love, reminded you of the cloud of heavenly witnesses, sparkled with tears of pity for your pain, and lit up with delight when you returned. Religion was numinous, smelly, deadly serious and ubiquitous.

Lately, the vacuum has deadened much of the sensory content, art has been deconstructed, language debased, time fractured into nanoseconds, history largely forgotten, and the eyes around you are all facing screens. 'Mere spirituality' is 'lite,' hygenic, lively and hidden from view. The fabric is thin. The road ahead is hard to see.

We need to imagine a complete continuum in order to create it; to articulate the path in order to step forward on it.

THE KINGDOM IS COMING HERE, INTO THE REALITY, THROUGH YOU, FREE

THE SUBSTANCE OF GLORY PRESSES DOWN FROM THESE HEIGHTS THROUGH THE REALITY ALL AROUND US. THIS 'NOTHINGNESS' IS THE GREATEST PART OF THE WHOLE, JUST AS YOUR ETERNAL SOUL IS THE GREATEST, IF INVISIBLE, PART OF YOUR BEING.

SPACE–TIME HAD A BEGINNING AND WILL END

It is important to keep in mind that the kingdom of God is emerging into the less–substantial reality of the world we experience in space–time and material existence. C.S. Lewis, describing the post–Resurrection entrance of Jesus through the wall of the Upper Room, emphasizes this point. Jesus did not waft through the real wall because he was ghostly and immaterial, but emerged through it "like a ship through fog," as the more substantial reality, driving the lesser away by its advance.

At some point in the lemniscate movement that weaves this fabric, it begins to be hard to tell whether the white line you see is a space between fine threads, or is a filament on fire with light. Form is holding open space for light, either way. The area that seemed 'empty,' is shot through with form that radiates light. The area that was 'dark' is now woven of so many layers of such fine thread that light seems to move down into it, absorbed until you get closer, closer. Then it bursts into flame.

What does it mean to do this weaving? How can you arrange your life materials so that they fill with light? How can you take light, value, or ideal and place it into form, act, word, story, image, gesture, and gift? Answering these questions for yourself begins to reweave your own full spectrum freedom.

Of course prayer is always the first and best strategy. But it, too, must be integrated with the wholeness of You, lest it become an abstract mental routine. The recovery of your own sensory engagement with the world helps you see your path. Your reconnection to your past, your place, your body, your community, your capacity for reality, beats a small part of the path for others. Your freedom – to receive, to love, to voice the Word, to give, to act, to grow, to respond, to create – becomes a growing 'zone' of freedom. Lift up Christ's cross and build the structures from which His light will shine in the darkness!

What context have you ever have you ever been in that was 'thick'? Describe it.

Think of a thin context. What is it like?

Return to the list of life materials you made in Chapter 2. Pick a few and consider, for each one:

Is it a vessel for light, or meaning, or value? If so, how does that show? Who can see it? If not, can you imagine it communicating some message? What would have to change to transform it? Maybe it's a knot that needs to be untied, a wound that needs to be healed, a word that needs to be spoken.

"THE PROBLEM OF EDUCATION IS WHETHER WE HAVE A SUITABLE ANSWER FOR THIS URGE INHERENT IN LIVING, SUCH THAT WE CAN COMMUNICATE IT IN OUR LIVING. ... ONLY IF WE ADULTS HAVE THIS ENGAGEMENT WITH THE REAL IN ITS TOTALITY CAN WE COMMUNICATE A MEANING."

JULIÁN CARRÓN
DISARMING BEAUTY

15. Real and Real–er

You can think of the Continuum Arrow as representing the gap between an ideal and its realization.

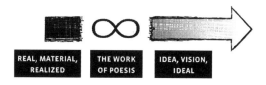

That's an important gap to close. Ideas can become daydreams and vain imaginations if they remain disintegrated from actuality. Without some capacity to imagine and accomplish new possibilities, life on the ground becomes suffocating. Ideas bring new light and new hope with them.

Ideas — a new story, a better way to purify water — and ideals — generosity, integral human development — raise the roof and so immediately a light, hopeful atmosphere results. This must be supported, or it can dry up, like a soap film left behind by a bubble. Often, the task of capturing the idea bubble in words, action plans and prototypes just pops it.

How do you close the gap? From the 'bottom' you must get some form around that idea, ASAP. Pray about it. Voice it. Write it down. Make a file for it. Use words to articulate the reality, the idea, and the path between them. Even if Step 2 is an impossible one, like "raise a million dollars", you'll have at least a map of the territory. Each step may require a map of its own. Down and down you go: placing that next concept into an increasingly dense construction of material, action, articulation, and commitment.

Meanwhile the bubble is threatening to pop every time you face the pointy end of another obstacle, of hard work, of not seeing the next step clearly, and of having nobody to help bear the burden. Return (the movement must be back and forth) to re-collect your interior spaciousness and freedom. Rewalk the steps that have brought you this far. Reconsider what the next free step is. It may be to wait, or you may find you have renewed energy for the arduous task of realizing the ideal. (I can't even recall how many times I've been through these steps to get just this book realized!)

The process of realizing ideas should help you better understand your own becoming. You are God's own poiema – His work of art, given freedom to participate in His making of you. You are real from the moment of conception, but also growing more and more fully realized as the glorious being He invites you to become.

Got any ideas? Pick one and quickly write about what the path to its realization would look like. Go crazy! Take big steps if it's afar–off. Don't worry about how you'd ever get those done, just (Quick, before you start over–thinking this!) whip out some indication of the path. Do it for all your ideas, great or small.

Which ones need inset maps for further detail? Files? A board of directors? An appointment with an advisor? Which one draws you, excites you, delights you enough to take its first small step? Who can you share these ideas with just to give voice to this imaginative content? (You really could email me! I'd love to hear.)

"FREE WILL IS A GIFT, BUT FREEDOM
IS A CONQUEST."

ARCHBISHOP FULTON SHEEN

16. Dynamics of Discipline

Freedom is a conquest. You are fighting to take and hold the territory of your own being. Your supportive infrastructure — like a muscle — is being built and exercised as you do the work of becoming free. As with muscles, you need both strength and fluidity, or activation and release.

My 'formula' for freedom provides both: "to wield yourself according to your own desires, and to yield yourself according to God's desires". Desire, then, provides the animating, opening principle for dynamic freedom; the energy that brings You, Free to fullness of life and realization.

If you think discipline is something better than desire — more grown–up, more noble — then you may have fallen prey to a corrupted idea of freedom. This false dualism prevents a great deal of reweaving:

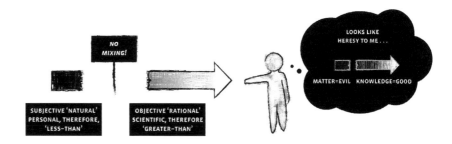

The free human person — his desires, feelings, needs, skills, accidental qualities, dreams, contexts — is at the center of the back and forth movement that makes him, not at the top of an evolutionary mountain.

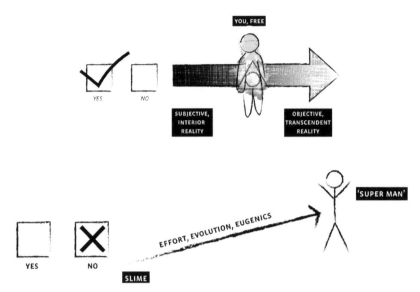

The quality of the work you do and the quality of the rest you receive (see *Souls at Rest*) permeate one another in the fabric of your being. The real 'mountain' is You Free!

The lemniscate movement–that–makes–you is a cooperation between you and God, between activity and receptivity. There's no room for it in the 'progress' model. That model leads to (at least) two corruptions in your practice of dynamic discipline. They differ with respect to means (in which we include matter, work, form, law, authority). Legalism accepts 'means' as an end in itself. License rejects, or has contempt for 'means'.

If freedom is the release from all the shackles of reality, from authority, from effort, then why bother climbing the mountain at all?

If freedom is unquestioning submission to means (subordination of the Self to the attainment of the Super Self), then we have only to ignore the possibility of a higher self in order to relax and enjoy life while we're here. A few of us can be Stars, or Saints, or Sages, and the rest of us can imagine being them. (Memo to Self: I'm not free unless I'm ME, Free!)

True freedom is liberty to be, to be receptive to God, to be ruled and limited and obligated, to act freely, to express selfhood constructively, to be an open channel for the flow of grace and the realization of Christ. Now that's worth the price of some discipline!

Holy leisure — its highest expression the Eucharistic Sabbath — helps set you in right relationship to discipline by pulling against the extremes of both legalism and license. Sabbath practice orders whatever work, discipline, effort or activity you engage in to your freedom. Without the means of grace (Sacraments, prayer, liturgy, ministers, Bread and Wine, etc...) your freedom (without form, authority, or obligation) may become impotence (the real, but limited freedom of an infant). Without the grace of means (living relationship with Christ, participation in the movement of the Spirit, real need for the flow of his mercy), you may find yourself merely tame — locked in a list of rote behaviors that do not support abundant life.

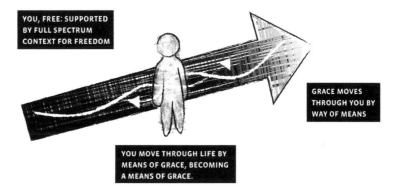

Judge your wielding and yielding by your own growing freedom. Are you working hard for some external reward, or is that work building your infrastructure? (If you can do it with interior freedom, it's building You). Are you relaxing into the deep ocean of mercy, resting in the wounds of Christ, yielding to the ebb and flow of the Spirit? Or are you just zoning out, escaping, and luxuriating? Is desire energizing you, energizing your wielding, or are you whipping yourself into action? Is desire energizing your yielding, or are you merely resigned.?

The first discipline is to believe truth. Then, to obey it

Describe the most disciplined thing you've ever done. In what areas do you lack self–discipline? When have you experienced the loving discipline of your Father, God?

How's your wielding? Are you energized by your own desires in the work of your own becoming? What are your desires? What all do you want? Could you want more? After all, God does more than all you ask, or imagine.

What does God want? Are you yielding to him with great freedom? Some freedom? A sigh and a shrug? With resistance, then grudging release?

Do you feel uncomfortable with all this attention on yourself, your temporal life, your bodily being? Write about that.

"SOME IMAGINATIONS TRY TO ACHIEVE A TENUOUS, MYSTICAL CONTACT WITH THE FINITE, TOUCHING IT JUST SUFFICIENTLY, THEY TELL US, TO PRODUCE MYSTICAL VISION, BUT NOT SOLIDLY ENOUGH, THEY ADD, FOR THEIR VISION TO BE IMPAIRED BY THE ACTUALITY OF THINGS. THESE IMAGINATIONS I THINK OF AS 'EXPLOITERS OF THE REAL.' THEY BELIEVE THE REAL CAN BE 'USED' IN THE NAME OF BEAUTY OR GOD, AND THEY WILL EXPLOIT PERSONS OR THINGS WITHOUT BEING PARTICULARLY INTERESTED IN EITHER....THE EFFORT OF THIS IMAGINATION IS ALWAYS TO REMAIN AS UNCOMMITTED TO THE FINITE AS POSSIBLE."

WILLIAM LYNCH
CHRIST AND APOLLO

17. The Excellent Reader

C. S. Lewis wasn't thinking of the interior life when he wrote *An Experiment in Criticism*, but his description of an excellent reader resonates with full spectrum freedom.

An excellent reader has both a capacity to submit to words and a capacity within which words may come to life. His interior spaciousness is, thus, full of supportive infrastructure. In him, word and meaning are nicely woven together to create a context for more words, and more meaning.

The excellent reader becomes a vessel within which words take shape and radiate light. He has not collapsed into the stories he reads, allowing them to substitute for his own vague selfhood. He is able to follow the author through dense thickets of words into worlds that otherwise exclude him. He has not only mentally processed the words as information but they have come to life in him, resonating with other stories he has read through literary allusion, and with his own lived, actual human experience.

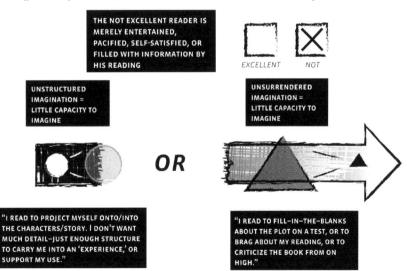

THE NOT EXCELLENT READER IS MERELY ENTERTAINED, PACIFIED, SELF-SATISFIED, OR FILLED WITH INFORMATION BY HIS READING

EXCELLENT   NOT

UNSTRUCTURED IMAGINATION = LITTLE CAPACITY TO IMAGINE

UNSURRENDERED IMAGINATION = LITTLE CAPACITY TO IMAGINE

OR

"I READ TO PROJECT MYSELF ONTO/INTO THE CHARACTERS/STORY. I DON'T WANT MUCH DETAIL—JUST ENOUGH STRUCTURE TO CARRY ME INTO AN 'EXPERIENCE,' OR SUPPORT MY USE."

"I READ TO FILL-IN-THE-BLANKS ABOUT THE PLOT ON A TEST, OR TO BRAG ABOUT MY READING, OR TO CRITICIZE THE BOOK FROM ON HIGH."

THE EXCELLENT READER IS KNIT TOGETHER, DELIGHTED, DRAWN BACK AND FORTH BY HIS READING INTO HIS LIFE. HE RESONATES WITH AND HAS CAPACITY FOR HIGHER QUALITY BOOKS.

EXCELLENT   NOT

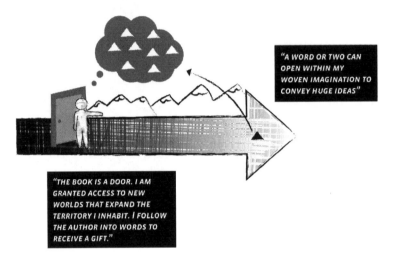

"A WORD OR TWO CAN OPEN WITHIN MY WOVEN IMAGINATION TO CONVEY HUGE IDEAS"

"THE BOOK IS A DOOR. I AM GRANTED ACCESS TO NEW WORLDS THAT EXPAND THE TERRITORY I INHABIT. I FOLLOW THE AUTHOR INTO WORDS TO RECEIVE A GIFT."

Excellent readers look like You, Free:

Neither full–of–Self nor empty–of–Self; neither withholding Self nor projecting Self; they are able to both wield and yield the authority of Self to the words and authority of an Other. They are able to exercise the imagination with fluid activity and strong receptivity. The excellent reader is thus free to read well all along the spectrum from simple delight to serious purpose.

Here's an example of a 'reading spectrum'.

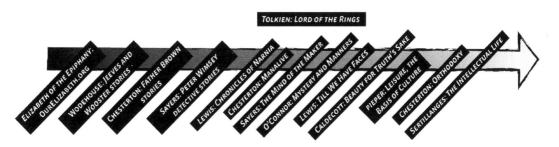

For yours, draw a big continuum arrow and place your own reading all over it, just to exercise your full spectrum thinking. (I'd love to see your reading arrow!) To make any spectrum like this just involves you in thinking about what qualities you want to focus on, what relationship do these elements have to you and to each other, what frame are you looking through that sets them in this particular relation. Does your spectrum go from humorous to serious, from child to adult, from earthy to spiritual, from worst to best?

"HARMONY OF SOUL CAN ONLY BE RESTORED THROUGH EFFORT, AND THE RESTORATION OF MANNERS AND KINDNESS IS AN IMPORTANT BEGINNING. WITHOUT IT, LITTLE ELSE IS POSSIBLE."

STRATFORD CALDECOTT
BEAUTY FOR TRUTH'S SAKE

18. Reciprocity, the Lost Art

A wrong understanding of freedom clouds your thinking about social conventions. Just as any infrastructure can become rigid, so with courtesies like the thank–you note, the timely response (s'il vous plait), and the phones–off–at–concerts rule.

Any form can become empty form. The greatness of man is that he can fill form, not just discard it. Courtesies serve real social purpose, helping to teach and enforce norms of behavior that make the civil sphere more a salon than a saloon. Turn from the 'figure' of the acts themselves to the 'ground' of the social fabric they help to weave, and you'll see that small gestures are among the most powerful to accomplish the recovery of the space where a free man can *become*.

EMPTY GESTURES– ACT WITHOUT FREEDOM IS NOT A VESSEL FOR LIGHT	GIFT BEGINS A MOVEMENT OF RECIPROCITY THAT WEAVES US BACK TOGETHER	FORMLESS IDEAS– FREEDOM WITHOUT ACT GENERATES NOTHING

Among the forms largely lost when man decided God was dead are these old–fashioned, meaningless, formal artifacts of a time when a hierarchy of values held open a large civil sphere for men's occupation. There, with these and other supports (such as many small, private associations based on locality or mutual interest), a man could enter into lively discourse, collaboration, conversation and self–cultivation with his fellow man. Made free by norms of civility, persons could generate a context that supports freedom. Absent that infrastructure (and transcendent values, and a sense of destiny, and the Church and God), the civil sphere has suffered great reduction.

Community has suffered. Social capital — the matrix of institutions *and* lived, or embodied values which hold open the civitas for the life of free persons within it — has suffered. None of us can rebuild it alone, but each of us can refill the old gesture, reform the old form, recover the meaning behind the courtesies. I suggest reciprocity as chief among these Lost Arts of formal courtesy, because I think we stand to gain so much by its recovery.

If I give to you (as a mother, an artist, a donor, a volunteer, a hostess etc…) you are unwillingly placed under an obligation. Try as I might to let you know how easy it was, how happily I gave, how little I care for repayment, you have a burden to discharge.

How does this accord with freedom? Can the two be reconciled? Of course, because it is impossible! 'Impossible' just means 'impossible without God's help'. If you are truly free, you have the capacity to do what you must, freely. In fact this is, possibly, the highest form of freedom. And how would you ever learn to do it without all the practice your life in community affords you?

The back–and–forth movement of reciprocity that springs from genuine gratitude for giftedness reweaves the torn social fabric to help it grow, again, supportive of the freedom of the persons within. Yes, your duty may be discharged perfunctorily, grudgingly, or as an empty formality. You may, of course, ignore it — releasing your interior tension, but adding somewhat to the tension of the social context. On the other hand, you may discharge it in freedom, with joy and creativity, and filled with the re–gift of yourself! The word 'discharge' brings to mind an electric potentiality that needs release. Something positive is implied when a tension ratchets up a virtuous potentiality!

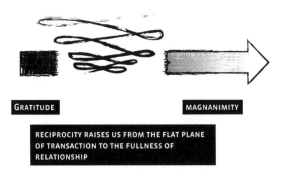

GRATITUDE　　　　　**MAGNANIMITY**

RECIPROCITY RAISES US FROM THE FLAT PLANE OF TRANSACTION TO THE FULLNESS OF RELATIONSHIP

Reciprocity, as a free movement of gift between and among persons, becomes generative of the context of community and radiant with the light of Truth.

That truth? All *having* is ultimately a gift of Love, and all *giving* is ultimately a response to that Love.

Has anyone been rude to you? How did it make you feel? Have you been on the receiving end of any gifts, courtesies, or forbearance? Start a 'gratitude' page in your journal and skip a few pages, as this list will grow. The more gratitude you experience in life, the more joyful you'll become. A heart full of gratitude is like a helium balloon, raising you up off the plane of struggle. From there, reciprocity is easy. Just let your heart overflow and, voila, you've discharged the virtue, the power, of obligation, freely.

That sets up a movement you aren't likely to control, so get ready! Reciprocity brings back baskets of 'leftovers' for every 'loaf' you give. Of course, if you don't want to be blessed.....

"ART IS THE HABIT OF THE ARTIST; AND HABITS HAVE TO BE ROOTED DEEP IN THE WHOLE PERSONALITY. THEY HAVE TO BE CULTIVATED LIKE ANY OTHER HABIT, OVER A LONG PERIOD OF TIME, BY EXPERIENCE; AND TEACHING ANY KIND OF WRITING IS LARGELY A MATTER OF HELPING THE STUDENT DEVELOP THE HABIT OF ART. I THINK THIS IS MORE THAN JUST A DISCIPLINE, ALTHOUGH IT IS THAT; I THINK IT IS A WAY OF LOOKING AT THE CREATED WORLD AND OF USING THE SENSES SO AS TO MAKE THEM FIND AS MUCH MEANING AS POSSIBLE IN THINGS."

FLANNERY O'CONNOR
MYSTERY AND MANNERS

19. Freedom and Habits

High virtue ⬆ is built up of many, many small – often hidden – acts ▦ of goodness, fidelity, obedience, self-control and affirmation of high values. Act is woven together with value as actuality becomes a vessel for meaning – in the form of You, strongly ordered toward your highest destiny, or fulfillment. Without realization high values lack the power they might have had to radiate light. Without transcendent value, acts lack the radiance that might have shone to lead others to freedom.

Virtuosity in any kind of doing also implies a sturdily woven continuum of acts ▦ evaluated according to an external standard ⬆: mastery and appropriation of some domain (fluency in a language, mastery of a craft or instrument, a 2400 chess ranking, a black belt in karate). Skill is the fruit of habits built into your nerves, muscles, and memory over time by practice, pain, failure, rest, docility to coaching and constant comparison between Where You Are ▦ and Where You Need to Be ⇒.

You may not be aiming for mastery of some skill, but are constantly practicing to become fully realized, fully free. This doesn't make sense without the reality that you have a telos, a high aim. That aim is eternal life in communion with God — divinization, as Christ will finally have become realized in you, through you. The saying "life is not a rehearsal" is true to a point. It's not a pretense before the 'real thing'. But a life can become a work of art if you make it a conscious practice and aim for all the goodness, truth, beauty you can hold.

Layers of value are woven together in you: Transcendent, eternal possibilities that correspond to your essential being; standards of excellence in the domains to which you are attracted, called, gifted and committed, that correspond to your effectiveness in those contexts; personal delights and desires that correspond to your own particularity. 'Practice' is the work of appropriating and expressing those values. 'Habit' is the freedom of becoming them.

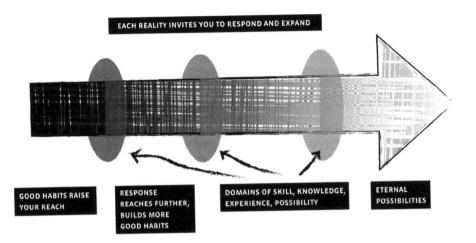

EACH REALITY INVITES YOU TO RESPOND AND EXPAND

GOOD HABITS RAISE YOUR REACH

RESPONSE REACHES FURTHER, BUILDS MORE GOOD HABITS

DOMAINS OF SKILL, KNOWLEDGE, EXPERIENCE, POSSIBILITY

ETERNAL POSSIBILITIES

As your practice knits you together in correspondence with the realities you encounter, you grow in essentiality, effectiveness, and particularity. Without this further development, you may find yourself with, still, a little gap in the fabric of your own being. For some, it may be quite enough to aim for holiness alone, without thought to effectiveness or personal particularity. For most, though, the form of self is woven into a thicker, coarser fabric.

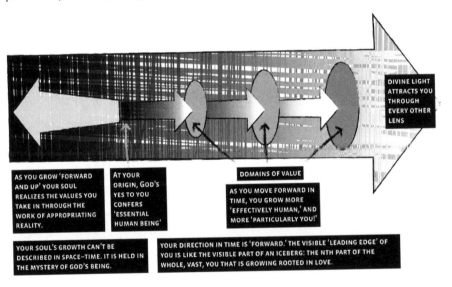

DIVINE LIGHT ATTRACTS YOU THROUGH EVERY OTHER LENS

AS YOU GROW 'FORWARD AND UP' YOUR SOUL REALIZES THE VALUES YOU TAKE IN THROUGH THE WORK OF APPROPRIATING REALITY.

AT YOUR ORIGIN, GOD'S YES TO YOU CONFERS 'ESSENTIAL HUMAN BEING'

DOMAINS OF VALUE

AS YOU MOVE FORWARD IN TIME, YOU GROW MORE 'EFFECTIVELY HUMAN,' AND MORE 'PARTICULARLY YOU!'

YOUR SOUL'S GROWTH CAN'T BE DESCRIBED IN SPACE–TIME. IT IS HELD IN THE MYSTERY OF GOD'S BEING.

YOUR DIRECTION IN TIME IS 'FORWARD.' THE VISIBLE 'LEADING EDGE' OF YOU IS LIKE THE VISIBLE PART OF AN ICEBERG: THE NTH PART OF THE WHOLE, VAST, YOU THAT IS GROWING ROOTED IN LOVE.

The light that shines through a Holy Soul, whether thin of earthy particularity or thick with trials and personality and detail, is a beacon for others, attracting them to higher ground. When it is more closely veiled in lowliness, pain, circumstance, and particularity, though, it may pierce more deeply into the depths of the surrounding Darkness. God weaves us all together for good, so I have no doubt every one of us, all along the spectrum, is making a contribution.

SOME PEOPLE SEEM ALMOST ANGELIC . . . AND THEN, THERE'S ME . . .

The work of your growing interior dimension, your expanding capacity to bear and respond to tension, and your radiant, emerging particularity is the very *way* transcendent light is woven down into the deepest depths of your being.

The role of habit in weaving you together is enormous. Habits are the warp on the loom! Their strength lies in making automatic some pattern that works well, freeing energy and attention for focus on developing new patterns, building on old ones, gaining new territory. Their weakness is their invisibility. Allow the Spirit access to all, though, and you'll see when habits need to change.

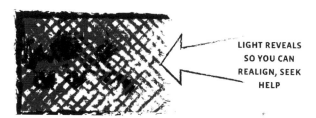

LIGHT REVEALS
SO YOU CAN
REALIGN, SEEK
HELP

Each pass of light may expose some knots, some threads that are frayed, and some changes needed in the underlying warp threads.

Habits that 'hold light' have meaning, embody values and intention, strengthen your capacity for freedom. Keep saying yes to these. (Your conscious, free 'yes' helps prevent them becoming empty of meaning.) Habits that just 'hold on' may have had temporary value (like a self–defense response or an efficient driving route), but if they constrict and twist the fabric, just say no to these

List all your habits, routines, patterns and self–management systems, or protocols. Check through the list with a 'freedom meter' to see which ones have become rote, or empty (mark those with an O); those which reduce your effectiveness, or are leftover constraints that are no longer needed (mark with an X) and those which add ease to your workflow, free up time for things you value, reduce friction, or are otherwise genuinely helpful, (+). Make it a point to release those X habits, refill those O habits, and say a conscious YES to those + habits. One at a time, please. Don't bite off more than you can weave into integration.

"ARISE, SHINE; FOR YOUR LIGHT HAS COME,
AND THE GLORY OF THE LORD HAS RISEN
UPON YOU."

ISAIAH 60:1

20. Knots and Healing

So, you've got the idea: light is passing back and forth through you to smooth and straighten the weave. Life material is building up gradually to become form and filament for radiating that light. Old wounds can be knots, or rents in the fabric of being. What's done is done, but since this is a living fabric, the past continues to affect and shape the future through the present. You might say it is a sound that continues to ripple out, or echo forth over the context of being.

If you move forward only as, or in a straight line, the possible future is more and more determined by the past. Each event, each act can shape, bend, deform, and prevent another swath of possibilities, so the path seems to grow constricted, fated, inevitable.

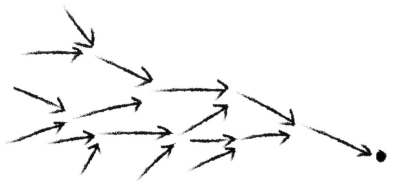

If, however, you approach your destiny in correspondence with the reality that the Spirit of God is moving back and forth to weave you together as You, then you realize tremendous new possibilities for recovery from missteps.

Yes, you were wounded on *this* day, made a stupid decision on *that* day, sinned on all *those* days and don't really feel much desire for holiness today. Those things matter — they are real, they make a difference in the fabric of your being and the narrative of your life. But they are not the only reality.

Also real is the fact that participation in, surrender to the lemniscate movement of the Spirit makes possible a real reweaving and renewal. The Great Physician heals, the Spirit unties knots, the Son within you keeps realigning you. No past, no damage, no obstacle is greater than the Love who made you and who holds you in being. He offers you freedom that you, alone, may close your soul to Him. What an enormous response–ability!

In every moment His mercy is new! His light can enter wounds so deep and time so far past and fabric so hopelessly twisted that you cannot even imagine how it could happen. But it does!

He doesn't change the facts, but completely transforms their meaning, their implications, or power to shift the whole fabric into a mess. The reality you face may not change, but your relationship to it changes. The accidents, or temporal surface are revealed to be mere background to the 'figure' emerging through them of an essential, eternal reality. What you offer to the Holy Spirit as fact, form, reality becomes a vessel for light.

Mercy is Love moving to the lowest, smallest, darkest place, to set you free.

The tenderness of that merciful love to pierce through to the place where you need His touch, without violating you, cannot be overestimated. Therapists, helping patients overcome the ongoing, residual effects of severe trauma, describe a healing process that involves gentle, carefully modulated return to the experience. Not all at once is the victim to relive the unbearable reality, but in a back–and–forth movement that allows the barest touch and its pain to be woven forward into resolution, consciousness, release, voicing, and narrative. Gradually, the torn fabric of being is gently rewoven over time, as tiny amounts of the burden are mixed into the person's being in bearable doses.

Time is permeable to Light, to Love. Your healing began before you realized you needed it. Can you surrender to the tender, rocking motion of the Spirit who broods over you to weave you into being?

How many knots and wounds were on your list of life materials? Did you actually allow the Comforter and Great Physician to untie and to heal those, or are you holding them at arm's length (maybe further — behind a big "I'm fine" fence)?

It's none of my business, but I'm praying you'll let the Spirit rock you gently back-and-forth to touch that pain, little by little. If it's not moving, it's not mercy!

"THE TRUTH IS THAT WHEN PEOPLE ARE…REALLY WILD WITH FREEDOM AND INVENTION, THEY ALWAYS MUST, AND THEY ALWAYS DO, CREATE INSTITUTIONS."

G. K. CHESTERTON

21. Context and Content

We can become fixated on content and thus grow increasingly blind to context; focus on problems and miss the whole reality; attentive to hot fires in the foreground while pretending away more important issues in the background. For example:

1. "My life is filled with good deeds and pious practices." (Yes, but is your life an expression of joy, love, peace?)

2. "My message is full of true statements." (Yes but have you carefully designed it to connect with and be accessible to your audience?)

3. "I feed my family." (Yes, but do you dine together? In peace? With meaningful conversation? Surrounded by Beauty?)

4. "I get my work done." (Yes, but with true interior freedom?)

The content may be ⬜➡ – value, idea, goal, truth, or ⬛ – food, money, words, acts.

As always, the task is to weave a context that supports, supplements and specifies the content.

SUPPORTS

The context is in alignment with, in congruity with, the content instead of fighting it – as when a path is laid along the lines walkers naturally take, and as when holy leisure prepares the soul to receive Christ.

SUPPLEMENTS

The context provides additional quality, flourish and flare, attraction — as a garment drapes a woman, or as an aroma accompanies a rose.

SPECIFIES

The context links the content to the realities of time, place, person — as when a medicine is prescribed for a specific person at a dosage that corresponds to his weight, and as when a judge instructs the jury to eliminate hearsay evidence from consideration.

Consider the need for context in the examples above.

1. A LIFE OF GOOD DEEDS WITHOUT JOY LOOKS LIKE THIS:

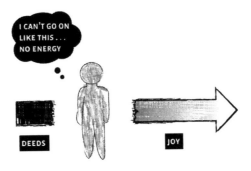

A context supportive of those good deeds would be the practice of holy leisure, of Sabbath-keeping, of drawing boundaries around doing so as to support being.

A supplemental context might bring more delight to the task (whistle while you work; make it a game), more Beauty (hand out flowers with the sandwiches, light a candle and sing night prayer; add a live band to your soup kitchen and art supplies to your homeless shelter), more companionship (take a pal to the nursing home with you), more prayer (pray the Divine Mercy while you sit at the bedside; offer every Mass for someone you serve), or more fun (Chess anyone? Can you juggle? How could you surprise them?).

Greater contextual specification, here, would involve feedback from others (your spiritual director, spouse, teammates) about how these activities are working for you, for the family; how relationships and finances are being affected; how well these activities match your skills, energy level and calling.

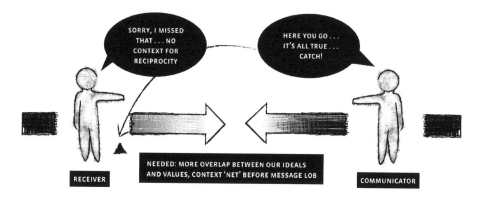

'Supportive context' involves your attention in consideration of the best place to offer it, the best media to use, the careful choice of words.

A message doesn't exist in a vacuum, but is carried on and in voice, text, handwriting, person, place. It is supplemented by qualities such as love, passion, kindness, and freedom, that all come from the heart's engagement. The preparation of your heart changes the context we call 'tone of voice'. Emojis are a thin attempt to rebuild emotional context in impersonal text/virtual exchanges. You may also want to add supplemental context by adding artwork to the mailing envelope, poetry to your speech, metaphors to your explanation, or kneeling to your proposal.

The specifics of message communication are the persons involved — consideration of what words will offend, or polarize the exchange, what might trigger a defensive reaction, how to offer truth diplomatically without violating a confidence, or what apology needs to be made first to clear the air between you.

3. WHAT IS THE 'CONTEXT' OF FOOD?

Recalling that 'context' asks you to broaden and expand your focus, consider the many elements that are, ideally, woven into us through the intimacy and essentiality of eating.

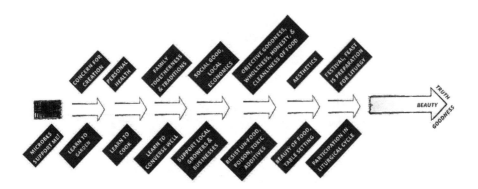

Look at all you miss if you 'just eat'! Food is, arguably, the single most powerful physical form–fillable–with–light, as witness our Lord's choice to become Bread. How wide is your gap between food–as–content and food–richly–contextualized?

4. How are you working?

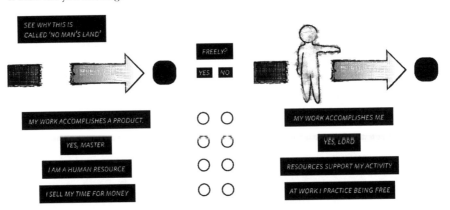

Notice that, as we expand 'content' to hold more light, we ask about qualities. Quality of action is expressed in adverbs. Quality of things is expressed in adjectives. These are verbal flourishes, extras not strictly needed, but superfluous. Man himself is not whole until he wears the mantle of his own superfluity! You are not free until you correspond to the reality that you are meant to shine with the quality of freedom, to participate in God's characteristic love and magnanimity, to overflow with the joy of knowing Him.

The quality of your working has everything to do with your becoming. If you work as an organization man, a house slave, or a prisoner, the weave of your fabric is slack. You are disconnected from your own destiny. 'Context' can help.

Free acts build actors. Unfree acts build only products. Freedom must be the interior context of your work, or you will lose by it. As you grow in interior freedom, your freedom becomes a zone of strength around you, expanding with every free act (and, sadly, deteriorating with every unfree act). Your sphere of response–ability is this zone of freedom by which you take and hold the territory of self. Your work and other free acts build your freedom muscles so you can take more. The single greatest context you can enter for the support of your freedom is the Real Presence of Christ — to adore him, to worship him, to converse with him to receive him again and again into your own being is the opportunity offered in the Eucharistic Sabbath.

EXERCISE

Pick one of the contexts you inhabit from the diagram you made in Chapter 6. What is the 'content' there?

> For example: the 'content' of my book study group is the book, and the discussion about it; of my choral group: the music, the work of rehearsal; of my home: the rooms, the stuff, the people who live and visit here, the work of maintenance.

Go through the 'weave better context' steps just for this one example. Imagine everything you can — you don't have to do it all, because you are free! Write about what supports and supplements and specifies this content.

> For example: In the context of a choral group, the piano and good acoustics support the rehearsal; the fellowship and sung night prayer at the end supplement it; the scheduling takes into account members' specific needs and the Church's liturgical calendar.

Does this context feel 'thick', or 'thin,' or 'just right' to you? Are you an actor, or an object in the background of this context? How fully free do you feel in it? What might be done to improve your relationship to it?

"GOD NO LONGER STANDS BEFORE US AS THE ONE WHO IS TOTALLY OTHER. HE IS WITHIN US, AND WE ARE IN HIM. HIS DYNAMIC ENTERS INTO US AND THEN SEEKS TO SPREAD OUTWARD TO OTHERS UNTIL IT FILLS THE WORLD, SO THAT HIS LOVE CAN TRULY BECOME THE DOMINANT MEASURE OF THE WORLD."

POPE BENEDICT XVI
GOD'S REVOLUTION

22. Dynamic Equilibrium

Bishop Robert Barron — master communicator and keen observer of the culture — has often commented on the extremism that destroys the civil sphere. Where bright minds should be conversing passionately in the service of truth, there is a wasteland, abandoned by the vast majority. Where are they? Hiding in forts of extremism.

Who suffers from this rending of the social fabric? Human beings, of course. You. That context was supposed to support you in the development of your freedom. Its lost hurts us all.

Bishop Barron suggest that we, free, Christ-filled, Spirit-led, image bearers of God would do well to become "bipolar extremists" to remedy the dynamic of polarization. Because we can perceive that this devastation lies in the temporal plane, we have a greater context within which to keep breathing, to stay whole and free: response-able.

To out extreme an extremist, you must look into the content of his words to find the values that resonate with truth, looking deeper into his ideas than he does. If these have become mere conceptual labels for him, you may catch his attention (even his admiration) if you reach beyond him into the greater context to actualize the inert content of his own position. He has become trapped in a position, and your act (words, gestures, art forms) invites him to become a free person.

GREAT VALUES ARE LOCKED INTO HIS POSITION, BUT HE NEEDS LIGHT TO SEE THEM. HE'S IN A BUNKER WHOSE WALLS ARE 'ISMS'. JUST OPEN A WINDOW

Does he value love? Show him Love! Does he value generosity? Show him magnanimity? Does he value peace? Lay down your arms and demonstrate interior peace. Does he want to protect his country? Give him a vision for well-woven territory with room for a full spectrum of inhabitants that is safer because of its great coherence and support for human freedom.

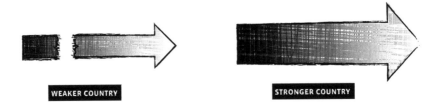

WEAKER COUNTRY   STRONGER COUNTRY

Another way of thinking of Bishop Barron's "bipolar extremism" is to aim at being an 'extreme centrist' — free to move back and forth across a wide spectrum of ideas and perspectives because of your own deep integration; centered by Christ within you; not operating reactively to fear triggers because held in a completely reliable Person..

Either way, you are helping to reweave the social context whenever you refuse to label persons, or hide behind labels yourself. When you are free to stand as a person in the sometimes-scary gap to meet with another person, you establish that unity-of-persons as a loom upon which high values may be woven together with words.

When you embody a high ideal in an act — gesture, words, form — you awaken something that already has a place in the mind of the other person, but hasn't yet been fully realized for him. When we idealize without integrating that ideal into messy reality, it can become an idol. Instead of breaking apart his verbal structures, fill them with life.

For example, St. Mother Teresa of Calcutta, vivified the whole world's concept of 'charity' and 'service' by demonstrating a supernaturally assisted servanthood. She filled the lifeless words that, for many, had become impotent substitutes for action. St. Maximillian Kolbe demonstrated — at enormous cost (offering his life to save another prisoner) — the possibility of a human freedom that cannot be taken by guards and barbed wire.

That freedom is the enormous 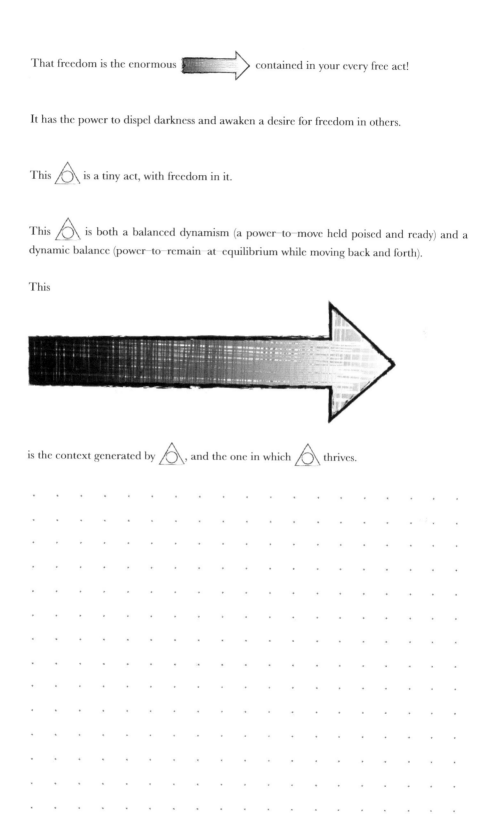 contained in your every free act!

It has the power to dispel darkness and awaken a desire for freedom in others.

This ⟁ is a tiny act, with freedom in it.

This ⟁ is both a balanced dynamism (a power–to–move held poised and ready) and a dynamic balance (power–to–remain–at–equilibrium while moving back and forth).

This

is the context generated by ⟁, and the one in which ⟁ thrives.

What extremes attract you, or repel you? Who do you know who is trapped there? How can you out–extreme that person with love and creativity? If you made a human chain to reach that person, who might be between you and him? If you can't reach him, maybe you can reach someone closer and ask for help.

Make a list of people you actually know who occupy different places, in your opinion, on some spectrum of beliefs, values, or qualities. How well–woven is your 'spectrum of affiliation'? Maybe you need to consciously seek to know a 'tree hugger', a 'right winger,' an adolescent, a Jew… whatever. Then, be grateful as God grants you friendships or connection with someone who is a mystery to you, and a challenge.

Beware if everyone in your life looks just like you! The pressure toward homogenization is great, and gets worse each time someone who does not 'fit in' quietly leaves the context that feels thin or unsupportive. We can't all be pals with everybody, but we can notice our own myopia in developing relationships.

"THE ESSENCE OF ALL ART IS THE FRAME."

G.K. CHESTERTON

23. Form and Freedom

The question *'What is form?'* has a lot to do with you and your freedom. Form is the thing generated when some ideal or idea is incorporated into material reality. As such, it is the content filling the gap between those poles, or potentialities. (St. Thomas Aquinas also speaks of 'form' as the pre–material idea in God's mind to which the material object conforms.)

The work of the artist is to turn back toward 'mere material,' or 'mere words' from the heights of contemplation, or inspiration, to do the hard work of weaving them together. It can be agony to take something so vast down into the limits of mere form without violating either, but those limits and that tension are exactly what calls out his greatest creativity.

Each time you make a resolution to act, based on a good judgment, you face the same struggle. The form generated in this back–and–forth movement is the means by which you are offered to others and by which you become a form that offers Christ. Recall that when we use a Continuum Arrow we've simplified it by dropping out the ⟨○⟩ person of You, Free to focus on the movement by which you – form, form–that–offers–you – are made.

God approaches man through forms — Christ, you, the Church, Sacraments — all means, or mediating structures. Divine glory approaches to shine in you, and also to be veiled in you and your forms. Divine glory also awaits you in all the created forms around you. Creation is not inert material, but presses in upon you, speaks to you of the Creator's glory hidden in its cells and structures.

What does any of this have to do with your freedom?

To be free is to correspond as fully as possible to reality — all of it. As you grow in freedom you grow better able to appropriate all the ⟶ that is offered you in forms such as words, persons, literature, icons, and better able to use ▮ to generate forms that contain and transmit what you value, what inspires you, and what contexts you inhabit.

You'll refill empty courtesies with profound meaning. You'll put ancient verities into new words. You'll be able to exercise a growing spectrum of receiving and giving, instead of suffocating in the flatland of mere transaction and exchange. The more you and the forms you ingest correspond to the highest possible Truth, Beauty and Goodness (not likely, but we must aim for the highest or the whole hierarchy of value deteriorates), the more will those you make do the same.

Your freedom helps generate contexts, forms, structures that invite to freedom, model freedom, and support the freedom of those around you!

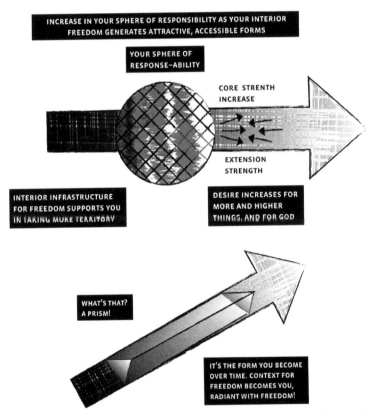

You are a form God is filling with his own image. You, now, could not possibly bear the weight of the glorious You that you are destined to become, much less the weight of His glory. Lucky for you, He holds up the whole of you while you grow up to fully inhabit the territory of Self, to dwell in it richly, and to radiate that very light through the stuff that is you.

Your freedom matters (literally…it becomes form)! What is the shape of *your* shining?

Have you made anything lately? Consider what little form you could make as a response to some reality from today, or from this week.

- Respond to this book: weave a little bookmark on a cardboard loom, with embroidery threads (so easy and so lovely).

- Respond to a friend's call for help: write a letter (yes, that counts as making), make a bouquet to take over, send a custom playlist of uplifting songs.

- Respond to your hunger: make an actual sit–down meal, with a place mat and cloth napkins and candles.

- Respond to those who serve you: thank the clerk for her smile, or hug a great waitress.

- Respond to the next book you read: send me that precís, blog about it, or write to thank the author and ask questions.

Act, word, gesture, form — it's what you do ▮▮▮ , so fill it with light and meaning ▬▷ .

"...THE WORD ASCESIS MEANS MAN'S WORK – MAN ENGAGED DIRECTLY ON THE PATH TO HIS OWN DESTINY, SEEKING HIS OWN MATURITY. IT IS WORK, AND IT DOES NOT COME NATURALLY. IT IS SIMPLE, AND YET IT IS NOT TO BE TAKEN FOR GRANTED. ... THIS LABOUR IS PART OF METANOIA, OR CONVERSION."

FR. LUIGI GIUSSANI
THE RELIGIOUS SENSE

24. Lenses and Desire

Fr. Giussani offered the helpful idea that you move toward your destiny through those things that attract you forward. Mr. Right comes into view, for example, and so corresponds to your yearning and to your destiny that your heart leads you into his arms.

ATTRACTION LEADS YOU FORWARD TOWARDS THE DESTINY THAT BECKONS. DESIRE SEEKS ITS ULTIMATE OBJECT: GOD.

Your interest in insects leads you through graduate work in entomology. The desire 'here', in you, corresponds to, or resonates with the object 'there' that is its fulfillment. Your innate religious sense — a desire for a More than any earthly reality seems able to fulfill — keeps telling you there is an Other, a super–reality who corresponds to and fulfills it.

Or perhaps it happens that an object 'there' knocks you for a loop, opens in you as new longing — as when Dante's encounter with Beatrice became in him a fulfillment of the Divine Comedy, which took form through him in response. Form is not inert, but mediates to you person, light, truth. A glimpse of his daughter's little hand all at once pierced the defenses of abortionist Bernard Nathanson, and helped release him from the stranglehold of death–dealing.

A little child is attracted to exterior objects. As you grow, your imagination becomes a stage upon which less concrete objects play. These, too, can lead you forward. Or not. When any object becomes an end in itself rather than a stimulus for act, the lens is darkened. Impure imaginations are, like lies, darkened by definition, and so shrink your freedom to ever–smaller dimensions.

The capacity of the imagination to correspond to realities both actual and possible is one of the greatest gifts to us from God. With a vivid and well–ordered imagination, you are enabled to build a sort of scaffolding out from the self–present toward the future–self that helps hold you in coherence over time, make and keep promises, and extend your core strength to support your reach for stretch goals. Your imagination enters the metaphorical dimension of human being, supplying a rich, attractive context forward and upward from the current manifest expression of you.

As you move forward toward whatever lens attracts you, an interesting thing happens. From afar it is bright and shining. As you move closer and closer, it becomes more full of actuality, partially realized details, and question marks. It can be hard to keep your eye focused here, as figure–and–ground compete for mental attention and close the view to the path ahead.

As you enter the long-hoped-for, attractive thing that has drawn you, it begins to loom as a reality. It may now be hard to see the light, the attraction. It reminds me of a legend about the three wise men. All along their journey to find the Promised One, they navigated by a distant star. On arrival at Bethlehem, though, the star seemed to shine directly overhead. They solved the problem by looking down into a well where, once again, they could make out its relative position, reflected in the water's surface.

If you find yourself moving into a lens, finding it different than you imagined, feeling its reality as a resistant force, or being confused about whether this actually is the same lens you saw from afar, look deep into the well. (See also: 12. Figure–Ground Shift) Find your direction for your next step (and your steps may grow quite small here, in this thicket of actuality) within your memory of that first shining, of the many confident steps you've taken to get here, of the desire in your heart that was a reflection of some glimpse of destiny through this lens.

When you've made that good judgment, (head and heart, remember?) act. By a succession of free acts, you'll appropriate the essential content of this lens, relinquish the accidents to God, and become free to determine the next move forward.

EXERCISE

What 'lenses' have attracted you forward? Did you ever experience the jolt of actuality as you moved further forward? Did you give up? Change course? Move through it to some greater good? What is attracting you now? How can you keep your heart focused on the light shining through it from your destiny?

"TO FOLLOW, THEN, IMPLIES TRYING TO UNDERSTAND WHAT YOU'RE TOLD. ...UNDERSTANDING...MEANS TO LIGHT UPON, TO GRASP, TO MAKE EVIDENT TO YOURSELF (OR AT LEAST TO GLIMPSE) THE CORRESPONDENCE BETWEEN WHAT YOU'RE TOLD AND WHAT YOU ARE (AND THE NEEDS OF YOUR HEART, THAT IS, THE NEEDS OF YOUR LIFE, THE PROFOUND NEEDS OF YOUR I). ...BIT BY BIT AS YOU BEGIN TO UNDERSTAND, YOU NO LONGER DEPEND ON WHO SAYS IT TO YOU. BIT BY BIT AS IT'S SAID TO YOU, IT'S AS IF THE ONE WHO TOLD YOU HAS BECOME ONE WITH YOU YOURSELF. YOU FOLLOW YOURSELF. AT ITS LIMIT, THE EXTREME FORM OF OBEDIENCE IS FOLLOWING THE DISCOVERY OF YOURSELF OPERATING IN THE LIGHT OF THE WORDS AND EXAMPLE OF ANOTHER."

FR. LUIGI GIUSSANI
IS IT POSSIBLE TO LIVE THIS WAY, VOL. 1: FAITH

25. Reflection and Translation

Like the imagination, a living mirror extends the boundary of Self, in a sense. When you see yourself reflected in an other — beheld, loved, true — you're being is supported in its whole movement toward destiny. A mirror can be a lens, helping you to identify smudges and surface flaws that need work. Only a living mirror — a person — can hold you in full personhood. That person needs interior freedom, integration, spaciousness, and receptivity in order to hold you well.

Too often, people living as mere surfaces–of–Self draw together with others who mirror only that surface. If a mirror does not lead you through itself to an ultimate Other for whom your heart longs, it becomes an obstacle — not part of the path.

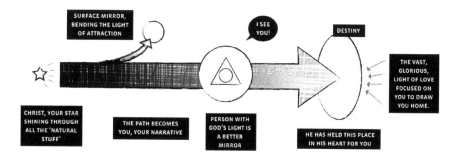

SURFACE MIRROR, BENDING THE LIGHT OF ATTRACTION

I SEE YOU!

DESTINY

THE VAST, GLORIOUS, LIGHT OF LOVE FOCUSED ON YOU TO DRAW YOU HOME.

CHRIST, YOUR STAR SHINING THROUGH ALL THE 'NATURAL STUFF'

THE PATH BECOMES YOU, YOUR NARRATIVE

PERSON WITH GOD'S LIGHT IS A BETTER MIRROR

HE HAS HELD THIS PLACE IN HIS HEART FOR YOU

The process of moving through lenses toward your destiny looks like a geometry lesson on the difference between reflection and translation.

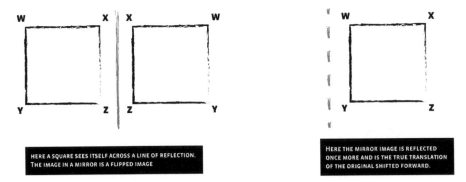

HERE A SQUARE SEES ITSELF ACROSS A LINE OF REFLECTION. THE IMAGE IN A MIRROR IS A FLIPPED IMAGE

HERE THE MIRROR IMAGE IS REFLECTED ONCE MORE AND IS THE TRUE TRANSLATION OF THE ORIGINAL SHIFTED FORWARD.

As a person, you need the depth of mystery of another person with interior capacity to hold (instead of merely to reflect) you. As you move toward your destiny, the various 'lenses' that attract you forward and up serve as lines of translation toward the truest possible image of yourself, held in the very heart of God.

Various structures help expand the territory of self, but outlive their usefulness. A new job provides a structured place for the exercise of new skills, for instance. A crisis draws you temporarily far past your sustainable level of strength. Music creates a structured buffer zone for the mediated experience of deep emotional content.

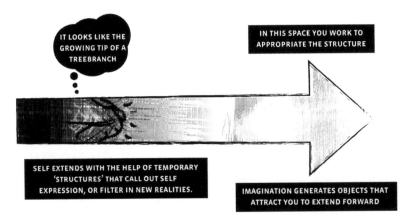

IT LOOKS LIKE THE GROWING TIP OF A TREEBRANCH

IN THIS SPACE YOU WORK TO APPROPRIATE THE STRUCTURE

SELF EXTENDS WITH THE HELP OF TEMPORARY 'STRUCTURES' THAT CALL OUT SELF EXPRESSION, OR FILTER IN NEW REALITIES.

IMAGINATION GENERATES OBJECTS THAT ATTRACT YOU TO EXTEND FORWARD

The narratives you build with your life materials are structures that contribute to your coherence. Even in sleep your mind links bits and pieces of disconnected, or loosely connected experience into dream narratives to 'tidy up' the clutter. On waking, though the temporary narrative collapses and may be completely forgotten, a bubble of meaning may have broken through from the subconscious depths to be better integrated into the weaving of You.

Your maturation depends upon the development of some capacity for self–reflection, self–inhibition, and self–direction. Your prefrontal cortex can be understood as providing a small stage for self–seeing — an interior 'line of reflection' for necessary self–awareness.

You, Free integrates what is seen 'there' with what is knowable only 'here,' by the heart's perception of self–held–in–God. Without that further line of translation, any of the 'staging structures' can become traps for the Self.

The story you tell yourself to explain someone's hurtful behavior can trap you, block reconciliation, turn on you in condemnation and bitterness, or be a lie that prevents you from incorporating reality in its wholeness. The role you grow to inhabit well can become too constricting to allow for further growth. Scar tissue can harm healthy skin and organs if not reabsorbed properly in due time. Imagination can project daydreams that distract you from action, or bend you towards sin. You can become addicted to the adrenaline rush of speed, fright, and danger. Music can become a replacement for the lived experience and pain of emotions. The gesture you once performed to weave real meaning into the fabric of life may become rote and empty if not continuously refreshed by conscious intention. The call of duty can ennoble you extend your territory, but only if you learn to dwell in that territory richly: freely.

Hundreds of advertisers are even now preparing to offer you not just products, but great 'experiences' lit with pleasant emotional associations. You are invited to step forward onto the stages generated for you by marketing scientists who know your longing for spacious places, places of belonging, and stories to project yourself onto. Their products are now props in little dramas starring 'you'. But is that You, Free there, or you reflected and stuck in a mirror?

The 'line of translation' adds the 'up' to your forward movement to keep your compass pointed truly.

Try this: Pray, at bedtime, that God will move anywhere He wants — within your past, your body, or your subconscious mind, to heal, to untie knots, and to 'pull forward' anything that needs your attention. You may or may not have a dream experience that seems to answer that prayer (journal about it if you do), but it's good to be in the habit of inviting God's courteous presence into your soul, life, being, activities, and relationships. Unveil. Offer Him access to bless and reweave you. You have not, because you ask not.

"WORDS…ARE EXQUISITELY DETAILED COMPULSIONS ON A MIND WILLING AND ABLE TO BE SO COMPELLED."

C. S. LEWIS
AN EXPERIMENT IN CRITICISM

26. Being Moved

Our Continuum Arrow can 'map' different relationships within the same reality.

For example, this diagram shows the movement toward integration of body and soul, or of brain and mind . In both uses the aim is a seamless weaving together, or smooth gradation between the concrete, temporal elements and the more whole and spacious eternal elements. The entire well–woven continuum is a picture of wholeness, integration, context for freedom.

Mind — still a mystery to scientists — is the context of whole–knowing that corresponds to whole–being. As a context itself, and not only as a quality of light, glory, or revelation being knitted into the form that is You, mind, too, can be mapped as a continuum.

WHOLE KNOWING = **GUT KNOWING** + **HEART KNOWING** + **BRAIN KNOWING**

What's being woven together to supply this rich context for correspondence to reality?

Whole–knowing — a capacity to take in reality in its fullness — involves your enteric nervous system, your heart, and your central nervous system. If you've noticed scriptural references to the "bowels of mercy," or relied on a "gut feeling" you couldn't explain, you've had a hint of this dark, physical, mysterious, deeply interior aspect of knowing.

The heart listens to and keeps in harmony the many different bodily systems, holding the beat of Self constant within a perfect range of variability. You need the mother–like counsel of heart knowing to form good judgments that are springboards for free acts.

When your gut registers some threat to safety, the self may collapse into a reaction (See 8. Your Standing Wave).

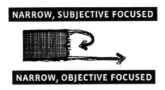

In a reaction, the forward and upward, full spectrum arrow of freedom becomes narrowly focused on self, or on the threat. If you can take heart, opening the gaze to more reality, you gently restore wholeness, hope, and courage. A prayer or song, humor, or sensory engagement can extend structure out beyond this pain, or this moment, reopening the whole spectrum of self and the context of hope.

If your heart 'breaks' or 'hardens' a real gap occurs in the fabric of Self. Without the heart's capacity to be moved, your body loses capacity to voice its wisdom, and your mind loses some capacity to render good judgments. Without the heart's courage (strength to stand), your defenses may be overwhelmed and your intentions to act rendered impotent. The "eyes of the heart" are essential to your relationships and prayer life.

Emotional intelligence, or facility, consists of freedom to move and be moved through a rich spectrum of emotions. Mirror neurons in your brain contribute to the whole–knowing of another person by replicating his gestures and facial expressions in your own being, so that your own gut– and heart–responses to those cues give you emotional and visceral access to his lived experience. Unless the sound of an Other can resound, or resonate in You, you aren't free to be moved by him.

Knowing can be 'shallow', 'flat', or 'one–dimensional'. The person for whom reality is experienced as mere mental constructs, or labels, has difficulty corresponding to the surface model he perceives. He is more likely to offer himself only as a surface to others, lack capacity to realize ideas, and make decisions that do not do take into full account his own deepest needs.

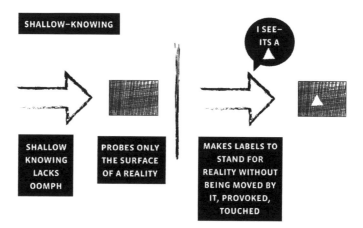

When the will is directed by a shallow concept of some good, there is no whole apprehension that can engage desire and passion. The arrow may aim true, but lack any energy of movement toward the object it knows to be good. You may find yourself leading Self along like a resistant and uncooperative child, or trying to shame and punish Self into going where it ought to want to go.

You might be surprised how much easier it is to act, freely, in correspondence with, or knitted–togetherness with the whole reality that is you.

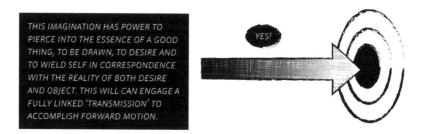

Similarly if you look at an object and then try to draw it without wholly seeing it, you'll find yourself drawing only a symbol.

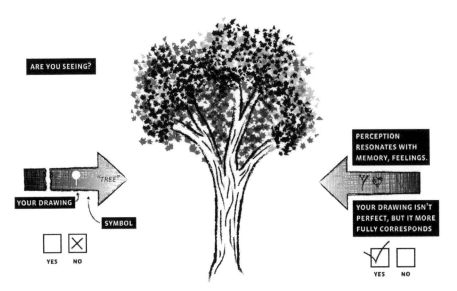

If you initiate movement without a whole–knowing that engages just the needed muscles via a clear intention, you experience what Alexander Technique teachers call end–gaining: straining with extraneous muscle action that develops habits of unfree, stressful movement. If you aim to produce a sound without actually hearing it in your mental ear, you may strain your voice, or believe the lie that you cannot sing at all.

Students who listen to a lecture, furiously taking notes, miss a great deal and strain too hard. Information rolls in to fill the mind and paper with words that have not been fully heard. Later, review of those notes does not recall any actual experience of receiving them, so the poor student starts from scratch at 2 a.m. Better to develop a well–woven 'net' for 'catching' them in your whole being where they can come to life, connect with other ideas and memories, resound with the teacher's passionate voice and move you to engagement by touching your own feelings.

This same receptivity 'net' will allow you to be struck and knocked off balance by beauty, love, joy — a delightful disequilibrium that reminds you life's goal is not to be immovable, static, or unaffected, but to participate in the back–and–forth movement of the Holy Spirit. To be moveable is to be vulnerable, but also to be resilient and undamaged by the encounter with reality.

This is the lemniscate, infinity–symbol movement of high adventure and homecoming, not the cowardly vacillation of the double–minded man Scripture describes as tossed by waves —, unable to know himself, find stability, or move forward toward his destiny. That insipid man is tossed about because he hasn't the *gravitas* of the full context of Self. He isn't a 'place' of coherence. He lacks the infrastructure for full spectrum freedom.

To open the gate of your voice, of your energy, take time to weave together a full spectrum freedom.

What person, subject, book, or city do you know very, very well? How much time did that take? The point isn't to know everything that well, but to have the capacity to place your interest 'there', hold that person 'here, in your heart', see the impossibility of ever thinking you could fully comprehend realities so vast.

Wield yourself to appropriate what you can, and yield yourself before the mystery and glory embodied in the forms around you.

Are you keeping reality at a distance by labeling it and filing it away in your brain? How long since compassion has moved you to tears, or music moved you to dance, or empathy moved you to give, or an idea moved you to create?

If you are always moving, you don't find the 'sweet spot' of interior calm that brings freedom to your action. But if you are never moved by realities that press in on every side to invite you into the Heavenly dance, it may be that you need greater imaginative power and less self–protection.

Your digestive system may seem a strange place to start for healing the imagination, but your microbiome is your closest connection to the created world. Loss of that contextual risk richness actually causes neurological trouble, and you need a functioning brain for imaginative capacity. How well–supplied with friendly bacteria, nutritious food, healthy fats is your 'whole–knowing continuum'?

"…NIGHT'S GLOOM MAKES IMPOTENT THE

WILL AND THWARTS IT…"

DANTE
PURGATORIO VII: 56,7
SAYERS TRANSLATION

27. Dots and Arrows

To be a 'dot' is to be compressed to near negation, but also to be very near the heart of God. He identifies most fully with the smallest 'dot,' because He bore, He suffered this near negation in His own being at the extremity of the Cross and the tomb. There, He meets you with resurrection power, to raise you to life. Suddenly, the 'dot' that was under all that oppressive weight simply opens to the light that shines through all reality. He doesn't become Superman, but somehow he's now bearing the weight of the world without being negated. He is reincorporated into the ground of being, perhaps at the low point of life. It may be a long while before he regains enough interior context to begin building outwardly, but the fact of his being — the image of God at his origin — already radiates. The reality may be dark, but his relationship to it is altered.

DOT CRUSHED BY REALITY

DOT IN REALITY

A SMALL SHIFT CHANGES EVERYTHING. HE DOESN'T NEED TO BECOME GREAT, ONLY TO BECOME REAL!

LIGHT DISPELS DARKNESS AS INTERIOR FREEDOM GROWS

The accidents may be what they were, but the essence has changed. The 'I' who was up against reality, crushed by reality, extinguished by reality, is now an actor able to respond to that reality. It is no longer an unscalable mountain but an upward and winding path; no longer an impassable obstacle, but a door; no longer an abyss but a deep well reflecting a star that leads you; no longer a tangled thicket, but a densely woven fabric of living narrative.

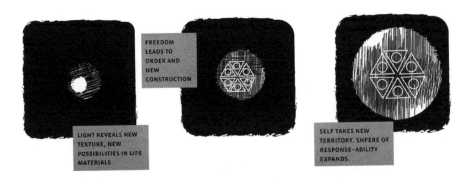

To be an 'arrow' is to be, if not crushed by reality like a 'dot', at least pushed by reality into some degree of compression, or disintegration. The 'arrow' may feel constantly at odds with reality, flattened by reality, tired of fighting reality. He's trying, hard, not to become a 'dot'.

The 'arrow' may be functionally better able than the 'dot' to act, but needs expansion in the freedom of his acts. For this he needs a shift from horizontal to vertical — toward his true north.

The context we live in, live through, can support and press toward hope, freedom, beauty, and spaciousness, or toward despair, bondage, darkness, and disintegration. We can't always change the facts, but even a glimpse of light shining through the dense thicket, or of some landmark rising in the trackless desert, or of some path aiming vaguely homeward can completely change the context.

I read the true story of a group of hikers lost in the wilderness until one found a map by which they found their way. Then they realized that the map wasn't even a map of the actual territory they were walking through! But to have something that seem to indicate a way gave them the hope they needed to move forward.

Your full spectrum freedom is valuable to you and also to others. You, Free are a context where others are held in coherence, known in wholeness as image bearers of God, linked to the various other contexts you inhabit, offered space to expand.

Your infrastructure may be their exterior scaffolding until they appropriate it. Your correspondence to reality leads them to trust in reality, and then to want the freedom to play in it themselves. You are small enough to be visible to those without much capacity to see bigger things. Your actuality — your real body, voice, struggles, personality, history, actions — gives particularity to all the high ideals and values incorporated so imperfectly there. In you another person — even with very different particulars — can begin to see himself. Just as a well-drawn character in a story has greater power to give a reader access to his own being than a vaguely articulated one can, you, real, help others realize themselves.

As you are more and more fully realized you bring greater order, greater correspondence, greater integration to the contexts you help to generate. How well does your home, do your friendships, works of art, your bridge club and soccer team and book group and C-suite and classroom resonate with truth, beauty and goodness? Those transcendent values guide the weaving all the way down to the picky concrete details of your life, where they turn your life materials into contexts of hope.

Dear Dot,

> Just because you are, you have goodness and truth and beauty. You don't have to do anything, or fix anything to win God's love, or attract His attention. You have a place in His heart, in my heart, here, now. He carries you inside, like a pregnant woman carries a baby. Simply rest. Be still, take heart, and wait for Him to shine through His image in you. It will dispel the darkness around you.

Dear Arrow,

> You are destined for greatness if you will face up to that possibility! You'll be alive eternally as you — within the communion of Love, in the company of every other human being and angelic being whoever said YES to God's invitation! You will shine with beauty. You will be buoyant with joy. You will have your tears dried and your questions answered. You will be cleansed of all impurities and healed fully. You are weary of struggling against reality with all your strength. You need His. Just ask.

'Dot' needs a little light inside to discover his own being. If he already 'speaks FoAm,' you can just say, "Don't be a BB!" and he'll understand.

'Arrow' needs a big light outside to discover the direction of his becoming. If he already 'speaks FoAm,' you can just say, "Aim for freedom!" and he'll stop to reorient himself.

Sometimes you feel like a 'dot', sometimes an 'arrow', and sometimes you're on top of the world. Write about some of those different experiences so that the symbols will not be empty forms, but instead be full of meaning for you.

When have you moved toward a wall and found it was a door? When have you moved toward an obelisk of pain, and found texture and a glimpse of light there? When have you felt crushed, buried alive, or trapped, until some small flicker of light opened your 'interior arch' or gave you new hope? When have you felt yourself taking and holding more territory? Just reminding yourself of these stories builds new infrastructure for freedom.

How about writing to your dot–Self and arrow–Self letters from you You, Free, to be opened at need? What do you need to hear from you when a gap is preventing good, full–spectrum communication?

"I TELL YOU, THAT TO EVERYONE WHO HAS WILL MORE BE GIVEN; BUT FROM HIM WHO HAS NOT, EVEN WHAT HE HAS WILL BE TAKEN AWAY"

LUKE 19:26

28. Meltdown

The airline industry studies every crash in great detail to learn the lessons only failure can teach. Lessons are emerging for other industries in which failure has potentially catastrophic consequences.

In *Meltdown*, Chris Clearfield and András Tilcsik examine the common factors of situations as diverse as a bank failure, a surgical mishap and a nuclear reactor meltdown. Three stand out:

1. The systems involved are highly complex — not just complicated, but so multi–factored and densely interactive that only computer models can come close to making sense of cause–and–effect relationships among their 'parts' (organs, employees, machine parts, financial flows, etc…).

2. The components are tightly coupled, or closely connected, so that activity or change in one quickly ripples through the whole system like a domino chain falling: one small touch and the fallout proceeds exponentially.

3. The humans involved must rely on intermediate technologies for information about what is happening, but often get so much information so fast that they cannot process it into a good judgment about what to do.

These situations interest me because they grow more common as more systems become complex (for example: a dam regulating water level used to be a simple system, but now dams are highly complex systems that require computer management through sophisticated instrumentation), and because they map onto the Continuum Arrow.

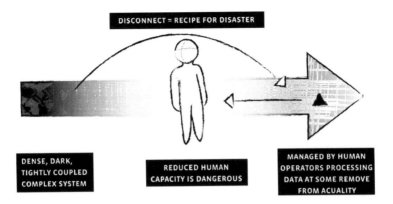

DISCONNECT = RECIPE FOR DISASTER

DENSE, DARK, TIGHTLY COUPLED COMPLEX SYSTEM

REDUCED HUMAN CAPACITY IS DANGEROUS

MANAGED BY HUMAN OPERATORS PROCESSING DATA AT SOME REMOVE FROM ACUALITY

For the most part, these systems work well. When the data does not correspond to the reality, however, or when a human operator is too overwhelmed by data to construct a response that adequately corresponds to the reality, meltdowns occur.

What do you do when you face a crisis of confusion?

Research shows that most people start by following procedure (like good habits, good training in protocols and procedures is a great help), then if that doesn't work (and without correspondence between reality and act, it may make things worse), focus narrowly on (and act on) one reason, factor, or solution (thus missing information outside that narrow frame of focus), or defer to authority (thus depriving the person in charge of a full spectrum of perspectives).

This is all interesting, but what really caught my attention is the way this research has helped prevent meltdowns. Communication is of the utmost importance. We may make better checklists, do more thorough training, add more fail–safe instruments and run more simulations, but we must restore the capacity of the human actors to act in correspondence with reality in the totality of its factors! For that we must generate a context that takes human beings into greater account. We must carefully craft verbal structures (even script and practice them!) by which the full complement of human whole–knowing and supportive social engagement and effective communication can occur.

No simulator can predict every possibility. When faced with an emergency, you — the pilot, the surgeon, the nuclear plant manager — need your humanity and the humanity of the wondrous beings around you to cope with reality adequately.

Time after time, disaster has been averted by well–trained human teams supported in crisis by a strong matrix of good protocols, good communication, and awareness that the situation's pressure to collapse them into human doings can and must be consciously resisted. The exercise of one's own judgement one's own authority and one's own whole–knowing must be cultivated and invited and shown to be of critical importance. The tendency to relinquish free agency to expertise, power, or authority must be overcome if lives are to be saved.

This sounds like good advice for maintaining full spectrum freedom under pressure: weave a context that supports human being.

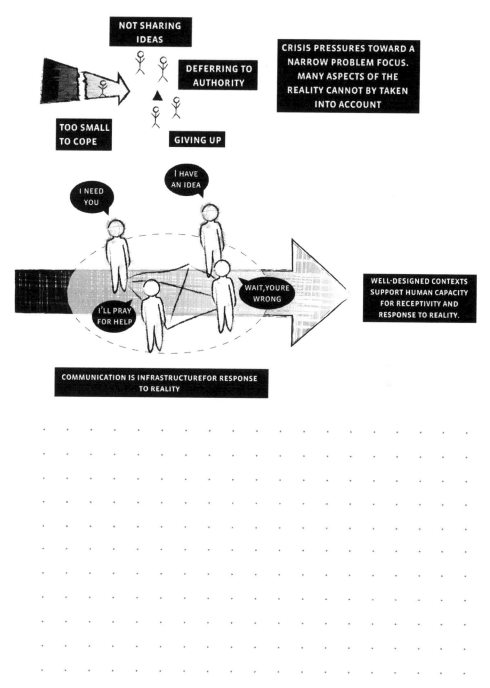

Search your own history for one example of 'meltdown'. (Was that hard? You and I must be very different!)

Write about it from the systems perspective:

What were the 'components' and how were they linked together? How were you getting information? When did you lose freedom to deal with what was happening? How did your actions push everything into further crisis? Who were supposed to be your 'teammates'? How did communication breakdown break down your capacity to respond? How would you describe your reaction (Going guano–crazy? A nosedive? A train wreck? Climbing the crazy tree? Going ballistic? Going postal?)

It's awful and also funny, in a 'nuclear meltdown' sort of way. All we can do is learn from failure and work on expanding our freedom.

"BEHOLD, I AM DOING A NEW THING; NOW IT SPRINGS FORTH, DO YOU NOT PERCEIVE IT? I WILL MAKE A WAY IN THE WILDERNESS AND RIVERS IN THE DESERT."

ISAIAH 43: 19

29. Light and Rock

While stable – even in slavery – the Jews lived within the certainty of the Law, rocked in the gentle movement from Sabbath to Sabbath. Stasis and safety are developmentally necessary for the growing child, the growing people. But further growth requires forward movement, in which coherence is challenged. The struggle to move toward freedom through a landscape without landmarks is central to the story of mankind, and of each person.

God taught his freed people to follow Him — as a cloud by day and a pillar of fire by night. They had to learn to look up, to Him, to find a reference for movement toward their destiny. Slavery had collapsed them into a narrow focus on the bricks, the straw, the work of survival. Today, screen time drags the gaze of chestless people down into a different kind of bondage.

Fully realized freedom, or full spectrum freedom, has three dimensions:

1. An essential trust in the truth, goodness, and beauty of being that can only be fully secured by being in, belonging to an Other.

2. A domain of work, struggle, discipline, appropriation where dynamic equilibrium develops between person and reality.

3. A shining Promised Land ahead where there is no longer any impediment to the continuous flow of provision.

In Christianity, the Hebrew use of 'rock' as a metaphor for the highest truth met the Greek sense that divine wisdom is 'light'. Through rock, the Jews had received the miracle of divine water, prefiguring the water of life flowing from the side of Christ. Through reason the Greeks had connected with the matrix of Holy Wisdom, as mathematics and geometry gave access to the divine mind.

In Christ, divinity and humanity were woven together perfectly. Super–reality permeates reality through His own integrated being. Christ established the immovable Rock of his Church as a floodgate for the flow of grace. In Christians, the light of His word continues to illuminate our every encounter with reality. Response is a free act by which your freedom becomes an open channel for the flow of the qualities of God into the world.

When man is a 'dot,' or an 'arrow,' a slave or an 'organization man,' an infant, or impotent, he is on the same plane with reality — duking it out with all the interfering, competing, jostling, impeding realities around him.

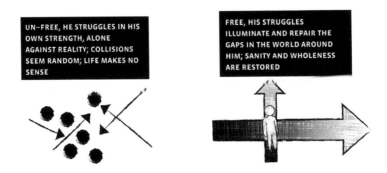

When he stands, grows up, becomes free, he becomes the agent of super–reality: in the world, but not of it. His words, acts, forms — no matter how small — change the world by opening the 'tap' for the flow of grace. The integration, or wholeness of his being served the world just by signifying the super–reality beyond, but also by generating new form.

So, yes, to the desire of the Greeks to discover the deep matrix of wisdom, law, ideal form and infinite number that lay beneath and all around the space–time continuum of creation. And, yes, to the longing of the Hebrews for eternal life in a flowing land that lay beyond the temporal desert of strife and struggle.

Jesus Christ — bearer of the water of life, and path, proof and substance of life — is the image-of-God-in-human-person who demonstrates how You, Free can bless the world. A tiny bit at a time, you are a reality-eater, reality-maker and reality-changer!

My friend just told me the true story of a man who cursed a disreputable establishment for years to no avail, but saw it shut down ten days after he began blessing it. It seems that to curse is to tackle reality on the plane of despair, but to bless is to draw water through rock, or to voice a new Word.

How many times have you voiced God's blessing today?

Scientists can understand matter and energy, but not explain what greater, or more essential thing (Force? Substance? Context?) holds it all in coherence, as order and life, against the natural tendency of things to move to a low-energy, disordered state. Love may be what they're looking for — the quality of God's freedom in giving that flows from the interior life, or communion, of the Trinity, into the world through Christ in his Body: You, Free.

Describe the 'domains of struggle' you inhabit. Which ones did you choose, and which were 'givens'? Describe the path through each domain. What is the high point you hope to reach? Where are you now? What is the material of that domain? By what means and methods and movement are you appropriating it? How can you enrich your interior context so it better supports your growing freedom in this domain? How could the other contexts you inhabit better support your work in this domain? How are theory and practice woven together here?

"...ALL MEN AND WOMEN ARE ENTRUSTED WITH THE TASK OF CRAFTING THEIR OWN LIFE: IN A CERTAIN SENSE, THEY ARE TO MAKE OF IT A WORK OF ART, A MASTERPIECE."

ST. POPE JOHN PAUL II
A LETTER TO ARTISTS

30. Middlework

St. Thomas described a beautiful thing as having three components, or qualities:

INTEGRITAS: Wholeness: it is not deficient in what it needs to be most itself.

CLARITAS: Radiance: It radiates the logic, or intelligibility of its of its inner being, and impresses this knowledge on the mind of the perceiver.

CONSONANTIA: Proportion, or Harmony: Its dimensions correspond to other objects as well as to a metaphysical ideal, or telos.

If you have not yet understood yourself (or the continuum arrow) as beautiful, look again.

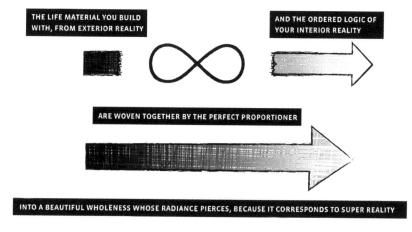

You, Free are beautiful!

I have a friend (you know who you are!) who always gets a bit tired of my high flights into super-reality and asks, "So what do we do? How do we make this concrete?"

Bring it back to lived experience here, now, me, my smallness.

So, my final words are my response to that legitimate demand that enormous things be returned to the dimensions, the actuality, the capability of the real human being, so that he may act to realize them.

- Bless everyone you encounter, every object you own and use, every bite you eat. Mentally, ask God to bless it, or — better — voice your blessing along with making the sign of the Cross. Engage the body, the breath; invoke the power of the crucified Christ and the love of the Trinity.

- Discover the Sabbath secret: the more you enter into Sabbath-keeping that is ordered to your freedom, the more its divine restedness will permeate the other days and expand your capacity for Christ.

- Get a clear idea of the destiny that awaits you. If you 'know,' but have no energy to work toward it, work on whole-knowing.

- Use words well, wherever you notice a gap, to lay down scar tissue, darn the hole, build a bridge, or throw out a lifeline.

- Don't try to pull anyone to any position. Establish unity in the Spirit, and let Him do the pulling. Meanwhile, just fill that space between you and the other with love.

- Connect with your body. It is trying to support your becoming. Figure out how and why you are neglecting it, shaming it, afraid of it, hurting it, unaware of it, not hearing its cries for help, or pulling against it. Notice your 'too slack,' or 'too taut' tone.

- Find some strand of your weaving to untangle and straighten. You can't suddenly fix everything at once. Instead of a house perfectly ordered, get one drawer empty and open it daily to experience delight. Instead of a complete education, read one book and send me a precís of 3–4 sentences. Instead of a perfectly kept Sabbath, choose a tiny, symbolic gesture (take your watch off on Sunday, use the beautiful china, or sit down and have a cup of tea with Jesus.)

- Get socially engaged; talk about this material; discuss your struggles; share your pain; work with friends to design better strategies; read together and have great conversations.

- Respond — let me know what you're thinking; write that overdue letter; voice the tension you feel in a relationship; bless those who curse you.

- Design good life–management systems, effective time management routines and beautiful rituals to provide structural support for your growing freedom.

- Adore God, pray, worship, contemplate. Repeat.

- Use your voice — sing, say "I love you" out loud, praise God out loud, read poetry out loud.

- Bring attention, prayer and blessing to every task.

- Go back and actually do the chapter exercises in *Full Spectrum Freedom!*

Describe aspects of your life that correspond to the characteristics of beauty. Some may possess and some may need that quality.

One last exercise should polish you to a shine. Follow St. Teresa of Avila's three steps to prayer:

Asking for God's guidance, take each of these chapters and your journal notes and

1. Read, chew on the words, get understanding, or brain–knowing.

2. Be moved, engage the affect, get heart– and gut–knowing.

3. Make a good judgment — a resolution to act on what you just appropriated.

Then, the final word for *Full Spectrum Freedom* is:

act.

FoAm, My Love Language

Here's the story behind my use of the triangle–circle 'language' I call FoAm, for *Fons Amicus* – Fountain of Love.

It all started when I was asked to speak to the Collaborators of the Apostles of the Interior Life about the beginning of the interior life. I prayed about how to discuss the early stages of spiritual life with people who probably had already matured quite a bit spiritually. Where there is a paradox, I look to the Spirit for a creative resolution.

I was inspired to try to recover a sense of childlike simplicity through the use of construction paper symbols and a visual metaphor for interiority. The talk really seemed to click, but the big surprise didn't hit me until much later.

In the weeks and months following that talk, I found myself, as usual, in a lot of conversations with friends that involved our trials and troubles. Over and over again, I recalled that 'triangle talk' and used that metaphoric/symbolic approach to illustrate all my wise advice. Concepts I used to find hard to get across were now sailing into friends' consciousness to the extent that we began to use the triangle–circle as shorthand for all kinds of related ideas.

It seemed I had hit upon an 'elegant solution'. Matthew May's *Pursuit of Elegance* explains beautifully what elegance means:

> *"…what sets [an elegant solution] apart is the unique combination of surprising power and uncommon simplicity, and that elegance entails achieving far more with much less when faced with a complex problem."*

May tells us that elegance is characterized by four qualities: Symmetry, Seduction, Subtraction, and Sustainability. Symmetry involves repeating patterns, beauty and balance. "Seduction addresses the problem of creative engagement. It captivates attention and activates imagination...Leaving something to the imagination, open to interpretation..." Subtraction is about doing more with less, conserving, adding value by taking away. Sustainability "implies a process that is both repeatable and lasting".

So, I think the Holy Spirit actually gave us an elegant language in which to speak of things human and divine. The symbols help generate metaphors by which two things – such as objectivity and subjectivity, or law and love can be held in relationship as an integrated unity that may be explored and experienced. Words themselves have always done this very thing. The addition of visual symbols speaks to a time in which, for many people, words seem foreign, complex, forbidding, or otherwise inaccessible.

From a linguist's perspective, a language is a 'real language' only if it has the capacity to generate new concepts and communicate them. Because FoAm does this, I confidently call it a language. Wives have taught their husbands to speak it, my kids find it easy to understand, and it keeps generating new concepts. It's an elegant, visual symbol system that helps us articulate and consider relationship dynamics and more.

Since FoAm is derivative of and dependent upon the English language, my task has been to clothe its visuals in just enough verbal structure to give them to others. FoAm itself depends upon an integration of its 'circle' and 'triangle' elements which is vastly easier in person than on paper!

I have found that this conversation, is very accessible even for people who are still quite guarded, or who don't usually reflect on and discuss the dynamics of their inner workings, or relationships. It seems to give them a tool, a vocabulary, for discussing the reality of their own disintegration, bondage, balance, etc....

It gives both metaphoric access to, and verbal distance from deep and difficult, or dynamic and difficult realities. FoAm, supplied with the user's own 'life materials,' becomes within him alive with meaning.

FoAm is a way of helping you draw on your own wisdom about what you need, what to ask for in prayer, how to respond to the realities only you face. No answers to problems are supplied, because they need to be voiced by you. Every book is a conversation in its way, but this one is nothing without that conversation.

I typically scratch out diagrams wherever I find myself in these conversations, spontaneously and informally. I've drawn them in beach sand, on frosted windows, on cocktail napkins, and in book margins too many to count. Since I speak with my hands, anyone who knows me also knows how to place their hands into the perfect, integrated circle–triangle when discussions lead – as they so often do – right back to a via media and thus, to FoAm.

Artists will groan at the graphic immaturity of the visuals, but Everyman will be able to reproduce them effortlessly.

Ironically, 'pointy' people are likely to look at FoAm and say how simplistic and silly it looks, while 'circly' people may look and see just 'too many words'. You can't win 'em all!

We who 'speak FoAm' might consider ourselves, then, a small 'community of practice.' As the 'hub' of what I hope will be a growing number of people in that community, I would love to serve as a collection–point for your feedback, questions, and further insights about You, Free. If it is a gift from the Fountain of Love, it is given to us, not to me. Please, please let me know what you think, what you experience, what more you need. You can easily contact me (respond please!) at CharlotteOstermann.com, charoster@outlook.com, or Director@ JoyFound.com.

Your response will make my day! Thank you for reading and being You, Free.

Examples From Practice

Members of the FoAm 'community of practice' have kindly allowed me to include some of their thoughts and experiences and journal entries:

> *"It would not be an exaggeration to say that the circle–triangle idea has helped me to understand reality—what is. I have been able to use it as a hermeneutic for life! Through it, I better understand what God desires for my life, what Christian freedom is, and what it means to be like Christ, the free and perfect man."*

> *"Letters I wrote in my journal:*
> *Dear Pointy Me, You scare me! I'm afraid you'll demand more of me than I can give…that you only value getting stuff accomplished…that you'll run off and abandon me. You get impatient and shift to a new game plan that would work if only I weren't there like a wrench in the gears.*
> *Dear Round Me, Well, sorry, but I am impatient with you! You just drag and drag against the possibilities I want to see realized. I'm trying to have courage here, to act, and you collapse right when I need to be able to count on you. At some level I just don't trust you. I'm fighting integration because I feel it will result in my disappearance.*
> *Dear Pointy, Me too! I'm afraid I'll be destroyed.*
> *Dear God, where is the path out of this awful self–betrayal. How can we/I be safe here?*
> *Dear Round Me, Maybe you need to trust more that it really is God who is calling us, and I need to trust more that Christ is present within to protect us."*

> *"For decades, I struggled with crippling anxiety which robbed me of happiness and prevented me from doing many normal, everyday things. The circle–triangle language gave me the understanding of the freedom to which God has called me: to inhabit and expand my interior spaciousness in situations that made me feel constricted and afraid, and to assert the boundary of my being, that I should never violate myself in an attempt to overcome my anxiety. By choosing tiny acts of freedom in difficult, anxiety–provoking situations—truly only offering what I could offer in freedom—I was gradually released from many of my gripping fears. I learned to employ physical techniques to*

bring myself back into balance. I can truly say that You, Free has helped me to embrace God's call to freedom."

"I had been deeply wounded by a family member, which was causing great anxiety and anger in my life. When the ideas of You, Free were introduced to me, I was set down a path of healing. First, I learned to create healthy boundaries in my relationship with this person. In all of our interactions, I was guided by the knowledge that my own growth in interior freedom could call him to greater freedom and that we could, through God's grace, grow toward wholeness and a rehabilitated relationship. Then I started to offer only what I could offer in freedom: I prayed for the desire to forgive him and to want to want to pray for him. Over time, God gave me the capacity for these things. I can now say that this relationship is largely healed and that I have been brought to a place of wholeness and freedom in my being."

"The counsel of a friend using FoAm helped me see that just one person in a relationship can make a big difference. Being response-able doesn't mean I'm to blame for everything. Being free doesn't mean everything changes, but I can sure affirm it changes everything!"

"Here's a sort of poem I wrote 'to' someone who seemed to be rejecting everything I offered. The triangle–circle helped me see this impossible situation very differently:
My heart was full of love for you. I offered it freely and you rejected it. You prefer the dark, cramped space of life without me to the possibility of being you, being free, being whole, being one with me. Where does that leave me? Love offers you enormity, but you are small; offers you greatness, but you are narrow; offers you gift, but you are too stingy to receive; offers you freedom, but you prefer the prison you have built. I want to be free. I want to be like Love, wounded. So…I'll return again and again to be offered, and to invite you to freedom."

"FoAm helped me with time management. I couldn't figure out why sometimes my systems worked and other times I resisted them. Now I see how I can lay out plans to take my circly–ness and triangle–ness into account better. I've been working with the circle–triangle language in my journal to get more integrated and reduce my self–defeating, self–undermining patterns."

"FoAm changed my relationship to food! I finally understood I was eating to stabilize the swinging pendulum and now I'm free of that."

"Thank you for helping with the dynamics of my marriage. I understand my husband so differently now, and have real hope we can grow better integrated even if he doesn't do much to help."

"I was being bullied and watched as you put words together to help stop the bullying without violating that person. It really helped to see you start from the circle–triangle analysis, then build a 'verbal structure' as you call it, to invite them to freedom. They still do it, but mama's got a whole new game plan! Thanks much."

Souls at Rest, in FoAm

AN EXPLORATION OF THE EUCHARISTIC SABBATH

Souls at Rest – An Exploration of the Eucharistic Sabbath could have been written in FoAm. I offer an approach to Sabbath–keeping that corresponds to your freedom.

Instead of a collection of prescribed
and proscribed activities,

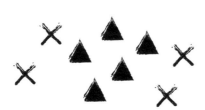

or a program of diffused inactivity,

I suggest that the Sabbath be approached as a 'tonic'. It restores you to freedom from either mode of disintegration.

As the highest, smallest, most powerful Presence of Christ, the Eucharist lacks nothing. We, however, lack much in our capacity to appropriate its gifts. The Sabbath offers a contextual matrix of support for the development of greater capacity.

The Eucharist is held like a seed within the scaffold of the liturgy – a richly appointed context for its unfolding, or communication. The Mass is held like a radiant jewel within the Sabbath day that can become, with your practice of freedom, a wide–open receptivity to the Lord of the Sabbath.

A Sacrament, and particularly this Sacrament, is Substance with Eternity in it, Law with Love in it, symbol filled with the very substance of that which it signifies, or in FoAm: △

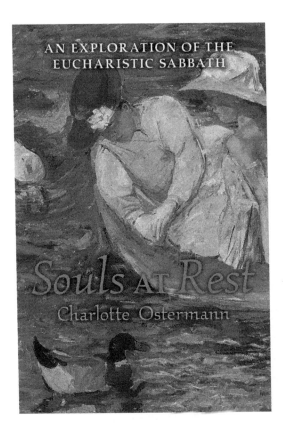

"I KNOW OF NO BETTER TREATMENT OF THE SUBJECT . . . CHARLOTTE HAS GIVEN A GIFT TO US IN REVEALING THE WISDOM OF GOD'S CALL TO REST."

DAN BURKE, AUTHOR OF *NAVIGATING THE INTERIOR LIFE*

ORDER *SOULS AT REST* (PUBLISHED BY ANGELICO PRESS) FROM AMAZON.COM OR THROUGH YOUR BOOKSTORE.

Souls at Work, in FoAm

AN INVITATION TO FREEDOM

Souls at Work – An Invitation to Freedom is undergirded by my experience using FoAm as a help in the practice of freedom. I define freedom as the ability "to wield myself according to my own desires, and to yield myself according to God's desires."

To surrender to God without fear is to open to intimacy.

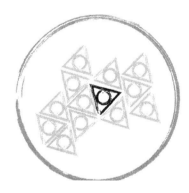

CHRIST, THE FREE MAN, RE-ESTABLISHES YOUR RELATIONSHIP TO REALITY, REALIGNS YOU TO GOD, RESTORES YOUR FREEDOM.

To wield the Self is to take the territory of Self. God's own Word stands within You, Free is the new and sovereign Organizing Principle. This territory is not your own, but is claimed in His name. To expand the territory of Self and to dwell in it richly, is to be free.

Souls at Work offers practice in bearing tension, in formation of the infrastructure of Self through metaphor, in engagement with the sometimes–hostile wider culture, and in creative resolution of the great paradox that your work is to become you, fully realized, through cooperation with the grace of God.

"…SELF–HELP BOOKS ARE A DIME A DOZEN, BUT CHARLOTTE OSTERMANN REINVENTS THE GENRE, GIVING US A BOOK TO LIVE WITH, TO DREAM WITH, TO WORK WITH. IF YOU ARE A TEACHER, OR A HOMESCHOOLER, OR IF YOU SIMPLY WANT TO BE 'FULLY HUMAN, TRULY FREE,' YOU WILL FIND WHAT YOUR SOUL NEEDS IN CHARLOTTE'S GENTLE WISDOM."

STRATFORD CALDECOTT, AUTHOR OF *BEAUTY FOR TRUTH'S SAKE*

ORDER *SOULS AT WORK* (PUBLISHED BY ANGELICO PRESS) FROM AMAZON.COM OR THROUGH YOUR BOOKSTORE.

Topical Cross–Reference

APPROPRIATION
8. Your Standing Wave
19. Freedom & Habits
23. Form & Freedom
29. Light & Rock

ART/BEAUTY/POESIS
4. Chiastic Formation
5. The Arrow of Progress
15. Real & Real–er
18. Reciprocity, the Lost Art
19. Freedom & Habits
21. Context & Content
23. Form & Freedom
27. Dots & Arrows

ATTRACTION
1. Invisible Territory
2. Fear of the Dark
19. Freedom & Habits
21. Context & Content
24. Lenses & Desire

BODY/HEALTH
8. Your Standing Wave
13. Full Spectrum Voice
18. Reciprocity, the Lost Art
20. Knots & Healing
21. Context & Content
26. Being Moved

CAPACITY/SPACIOUSNESS
6. About Growth
7. Tense & Tension
8. Your Standing Wave
9. Step–Down Transformation
13. Full Spectrum Voice
17. The Excellent Reader
18. Reciprocity, the Lost Art

19. Freedom & Habits
25. Reflection & Translation
26. Being Moved
27. Dots & Arrows
28. Meltdown

CHRIST
1. Invisible Territory
5. The Arrow of Progress
7. Tense & Tension
12. Figure–Ground Shift
16. Dynamics of Discipline
21. Context & Content
22. Dynamic Equilibrium
29. Light & Rock

CHURCH
5. The Arrow of Progress
7. Tense & Tension
23. Form & Freedom
29. Light & Rock

COMMUNICATION
10. Hierarchy of Value
11. Metaphor is a Way
21. Context & Content
28. Meltdown

CREATION
5. The Arrow of Progress
9. Step–Down Transformation
23. Form & Freedom

CREATIVITY
18. Reciprocity, the Lost Art
21. Context & Content
23. Form & Freedom

IMAGINATION
7. Tense & Tension
8. Your Standing Wave
15. Real & Real–er
17. The Excellent Reader
24. Lenses & Desire

LITURGY/WORSHIP/SACRAMENT
9. Step–Down Transformation
16. Dynamics of Discipline
21. Context & Content
23. Form & Freedom

LITERATURE/STORY
4. Chiastic Formation
7. Tense & Tension
11. Metaphor is a Way
14. Thick & Thin
23. Form & Freedom
27. Dots & Arrows
29. Light & Rock

METAPHOR
11. Metaphor is a Way
13. Full Spectrum Voice
24. Lenses & Desire
29. Light & Rock

ORGANIZATION MAN/MASS MAN
10. Hierarchy of Value
21. Context & Content
29. Light & Rock

PERCEPTION/KNOWING/SEEING
2. Fear of the Dark
3. Learning to See
12. Figure–Ground Shift
24. Lenses & Desire
25. Reflection & Translation
26. Being Moved

PROGRESS
4. Chiastic Formation
5. The Arrow of Progress

11. Metaphor is a Way
16. Dynamics of Discipline

RECEPTIVITY
13. Full Spectrum Voice
16. Dynamics of Discipline
17. The Excellent Reader
25. Reflection & Translation
26. Being Moved

SABBATH/HOLY LEISURE
8. Your Standing Wave
16. Dynamics of Discipline
21. Context & Content
29. Light & Rock

TIME/TEMPORAL
2. Fear of the Dark
4. Chiastic Formation
5. The Arrow of Progress
7. Tense & Tension
9. Step–Down Transformation
12. Figure–Ground Shift
14. Thick & Thin
20. Knots & Healing

VOICE/SOUND
8. Your Standing Wave
11. Metaphor is a Way
13. Full Spectrum Voice
20. Knots & Healing
26. Being Moved
29. Light & Rock

Other Books by Charlotte Ostermann

"THEREIN LIES THE NOBILITY OF THE FAITH:
THAT WE HAVE THE HEART TO DARE SOMETHING"

BL. CARDINAL JOHN HENRY NEWMAN

Ostermann takes up Cardinal Newman's challenge,
giving readers the heart they need to live faith as a daring
adventure.

Essays accompany each poem to make it more accessible,
allowing readers to understand allusions, invented words,
spiritual ideas, and the craft of poesis as they learn with the
poet to read, hear and pray with poetry.

The person of the poet emerges from the interplay
between essays and poems, as a spiritual mentor and
companion in faith. *A Destiny to Burn* invites readers to
experience themselves as masterpieces – *poema* – crafted by
the hand of God.

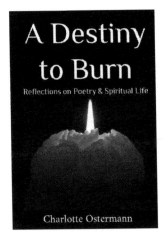

You, Free is a way of speaking about interior freedom in
an elegant symbolic language that gives cognitive distance
from and metaphoric access to the deep dynamics of our
mental, emotional, and spiritual processes.

This is a workbook for the practice of freedom, a seed for
fascinating conversations, and a scaffolding that supports
your freedom as it grows

About the Author

Charlotte has been weaving poetry and faith together for many years as a spiritual mentor, author, and inspirational speaker. She is the author of *Souls at Rest – An Exploration of the Eucharistic Sabbath, Souls at Work – An Invitation to Freedom, Souls at Play – Reflections on Creativity and Faith* (in progress), *Making Sunday Special, Life in Motion, Dare Your Something, Elizabeth of the Epiphany*, and *You Free: 50 Elegant Lessons in Freedom. A Destiny to Burn* is a collection of her published and unpublished poems, with reflections and reading notes. Some have served as the core of her talks and retreats.

Charlotte's poetry workshop, *Playing with Words*, has been custom tailored for retreats and workshops, and schools. Her poems, book reviews and articles have appeared in Canticle, St. Austin Review, Gilbert, Thessauri Ecclessiae, the Cardinal Newman Society Journal, and elsewhere. She is a blog–contributor to Catholic Exchange, Catholic 365, Roman Catholic Spiritual Direction, and Catholic Writers Guild.

Charlotte is a founding member of the Family of the Apostles of the Interior Life, the Living Poem Society, the Catholic Creatives Salon, Sursum Corda Polyphony Ensemble, and the Northeast Kansas Chesterton Society. She blogs, consults with non–profit organizations, speaks about holy leisure, education, poetry, rhetoric, creativity and cultural redemption, and directs the Joy Foundation – a small non–profit dedicated to Catholic cultural initiatives (JoyFound.org). Please visit CharlotteOstermann.com for more information and an easy contact form.

About the Designer

Cameron DuPratte is an artist and designer fron Lawrence, Kansas. A graduate from The University of Kansas in Visual Art, he now handles a wide variety of projects, from educational materials to music promotion, on top of a mountain of personal work–all of which can be seen on his website, www.camerondupratte.com.

When he is not working on his computer or covered in paint, you may find DuPratte and his wife feeding their many reptiles or playing Dungeons and Dragons with their friends.

MotherheartPress

Motherheart Press is a project of the Joy Foundation. Motherheart resources support Catholic families, Catholic artists, Catholic educators, and those who build Catholic culture in other ways. All proceeds from the sale of Motherheart books support Joy's various Catholic cultural initiatives.

Contributions to Joy are also gratefully accepted, and support such projects as Catholic book study groups, 50 Million Names, Sursum Corda Polyphony Ensemble, Most Pure Heart of Mary Catholic Youth Choir, Catholic Creatives Salon, Northeast Kansas Chesterton Society, Poetry workshops for Catholic schools, Chesterton Society's Digital Chesterton project, grants to Catholic artists and iconographers, Joyful Moms Workshops, Regency Guild dances, Jubilate Deo children's choir, a resource lending library and Bright City. Joy also sponsors Charlotte's speaking engagements for groups that can't afford speaker fees.

Several Motherheart books are available for free download at MotherheartPress.com. Charlotte Ostermann, Joy's Director, welcomes you to receive, participate, donate, and respond…FREELY! We ask that you do not photocopy or scan, but refer others to MotherheartPress.com. Your referral is more support for Joy.

You're invited to watch a brief video about the Joy Foundation at www.JoyFound.org.

FoAm—What's Next?

The Freedom Trilogy developed from the 'triangle–circle' to the 'continuum arrow,' and then finally to the 'freedom sphere'. They each generated a wealth of new insights and conversations. From those conversations come a language that we hope will be tremendously helpful in your own practice of finding, expanding, and enjoying your glorious freedom. Because it is simple and uses diagrams anyone can easily draw, it should also be of great help to you if you want to invite your family and friends to grow in freedom with you. Combine your own 'life materials' with the language of FoAm to create your own, personal, interactive course in freedom! Please dig into *You, Free* and *Full Spectrum Freedom* with pen in hand before *3D Freedom* arrives.

Here's a peek inside:

- Foam & Bubble Nets
- Trigonometry & Time
- The Turbulent Center
- Ladders of Proportion
- Spherical Spectrum
- Desire's Open Gate
- Immaculate Receptivity
- Sound & Story
- Fractal Fullness
- Self–Cultivation
- The Wholeness of Things
- World Weaving
- We, Free
- The Form of Freedom
- Interior Tensegrity
- Born in Wonder
- Approaching the Matrix of Wisdom

See you in 3D!